BIG BASIN
REDWOOD FOREST

BIG BASIN
REDWOOD FOREST

California's Oldest State Park

TRACI BLISS

Foreword by Martin Rizzo-Martínez & Mark G. Hylkema

THE
History
PRESS

Published by The History Press
Charleston, SC
www.historypress.com

Front cover, top: In the distance are Pine Mountain and Mount McAbee in the heart of the Santa Cruz Mountains. Below are Big Basin Park headquarters, campgrounds and trails. *Courtesy of Bill Rhoades Collection. Front cover, bottom*: Duncan McPherson of Santa Cruz commissioned A.P. Hill to create this oil painting for San Francisco's Pan Pacific Exhibition in 1915. Three members of the McPherson family admire the 1,800-year-old Father Tree. *Courtesy of Robert Bettencourt, History San Jose. Back cover*: Sempervirens Falls provides a soothing place to relax near the famous Slippery Rock. An easy four-mile loop hike from Park Headquarters, it is conveniently situated next to Sky Meadow Road. *Courtesy of Bill Rhoades Collection. Back cover, inset:* As a prominent Big Basin advocate, Louise Coffin Jones used her talent as a journalist and her leadership role in the San Jose Woman's Club to support the Sempervirens' cause. *Courtesy of the Jones Family Collection.*

First published 2021

Manufactured in the United States

ISBN 9781467145046

Library of Congress Control Number: 2021941020

Notice: The information in this book is true and complete to the best of our knowledge. It is offered without guarantee on the part of the author or The History Press. The author and The History Press disclaim all liability in connection with the use of this book.

For the women and men of Big Basin: past, present and yet-to-come.

CONTENTS

CONTENTS

FOREWORD

T he Santa Cruz Mountain range, in which Big Basin is a central feature, was home to several California Native American tribes whose people defined their homelands and territories through connectedness—ancient linkages of both kinship alliances and economic interactions.

This book examines the extraordinary steps taken to protect the so-called "wilderness" lands now known as Big Basin Redwoods State Park, which many would eventually consider the birthplace of the environmental movement. It is important, though, to remember that the Santa Cruz Mountain range comprised the homelands of Indigenous people such as the Cotoni for thousands of years. For them, this earth was far from wild.

The Cotoni and their ancestors certainly shared the same sense of sacred awe over the majesty of the redwoods that later environmentalists and the rest of us feel, but theirs came from an intimate knowledge and familiarity with the abundant resources available in these lands. The very idea of "preserving" an "untouched" or pristine "wilderness" was built on erasure, consciously or not, of the long history of Indigenous land management practices that took place in their homelands.

Over many thousands of years, the Indigenous people developed techniques for tending the natural world to increase its bounty. Each tribe consisted of groups of families residing in a few neighboring villages, and territories were largely determined by the resource patches a given community could productively manage. Tilling meadows to improve the growth of edible bulbs and the intermittent controlled application of fire were among the effective strategies for creating successions of diverse and healthy plant communities.

Among the many Ohlone language dialects spoken by the Indigenous peoples of the Santa Cruz Mountain range, some called the mountains Mak-Sah-Re-Jah. In historic times, the eighteen thousand acres of Big Basin State Park were the ancestral homelands of an intersection of tribal peoples, principally the Cotoni and the Quiroste, although mostly the former. The Rancho del Oso area of the park along Waddell Creek appears to have been a boundary (or mutual lands) between the Quiroste and Cotoni, with the Cotoni living south of the creek and the Quiroste to the north. The Big Basin park entrance sits in what is now called Saddle Mountain; this area was once the vicinity of what we believe was the large Cotoni village known as Achistaca.

Several archaeological sites are scattered along Ben Lomond Mountain directly above the park and provide evidence that Native people maintained patches of meadows and oak woodland within the park's forest; the finding of chipped stone flakes that were once used to cut stems and shoots testify to their gardening work and stone tool maintenance. The larger community of Cotoni people also had residential villages on the coastal terrace below the mountains, at Davenport and Scott Creek, thereby assuring access to marine resources.

The Cotoni were part of a wide-ranging trade network of shell bead exchange and abalone ornament production fueled by consumer demand throughout interior California, and the tribe was able to control the export of these commodities to maintain their value. In return, exotic materials like obsidian, used for chipped stone spears and arrowheads—from quarries in both the eastern Sierra and north Coast Range—were available to the Cotoni through long-distance trade connections.

The tribal people and their neighbors drew on the abundance of natural resources distributed throughout Big Basin State Park. From the annual return of migrating salmonid fishes, to edible fungi, sorrel, fern shoots and miner's lettuce, to hazel nuts, maple seeds, laurel nuts, acorns and seasonally ripe berries like huckleberry, toyon, manzanita and snow berry and useful roots like soap lily, iris and brodiaea bulbs (just to name a few), we can conclude that the Cotoni managed a wide variety of food plants that responded well to their efforts to improve productivity.

Intermittent meadows in the redwood forest needed regular burning to keep the encroaching Douglas firs and other trees out. This achieved two

Native dancers at Mission San Jose in 1806. Drawn by German naturalists and explorers Georg H. von Langsdorff or Wilhelm Gottlief Tilesius von Tilenau, who were accompanying the Russian American Company. *Courtesy of the Bancroft Library, University of California, Berkeley.*

important goals: these places attracted browsing game animals like deer and produced edible hard seeds that were milled between stones to make flour for food preparation. Marshy wetlands supported tule and bulrush as well as groves of willows that all served as building materials for their homes. Clearly, the balance achieved by the Cotoni and their neighbors in their co-adaptive relationships reflected an ever-present affinity to the land, their families and their creator. But that balance, honed over thousands of years, eventually became entangled in the colonial ambitions of a world that cared little for the tight affinities between the indigenous people, their lands and each other.

The Spanish arrived in the Monterey Bay area in 1769, founded Mission San Carlos in Monterey in 1770 and began the process of converting Native people to Catholicism and relocating them to the missions for labor shortly thereafter. The Cotoni and Achistaca villagers maintained their independence through this early wave, but by the fall of 1791, the Spanish had founded Mission Santa Cruz and began to focus on converting the people of Mak-Sah-Re-Jah. The very first person baptized at the newly founded mission was a young child, listed as being from the Achistaca village. Between 1791 and 1800, 178 people from this village and the larger tribe received baptism.[1]

Though the Cotoni people's lives were dramatically disrupted and upturned by the arrival of the Spanish colonists, they played important roles within the intermixing Indigenous community that formed at the mission, helping surviving members navigate through this time of incredible change.

In the years after the Cotoni people's removal, the dense redwood forests were for a time *terra incognita* for the Spanish settlers. They established several sawmills at various locations but tended to stay out of the woods, and various reports tell of mission fugitives making their way back to their ancestral village sites for ceremonies, dances and songs. In 1793, a group of fugitives from local missions gathered in Quiroste lands before attacking Mission Santa Cruz because some of the Quiroste women had been married by Catholic priests to men outside of their traditional marriage commitments. By the 1820s and '30s, Indigenous fugitives, such as the Coast Miwok outlaw Pomponio, were using these woods to hide out from Spanish authorities.[2]

The colonial occupation and rapid removal of the Cotoni and Achistaca villagers to the local mission helped to pave the way for the sense of pristine and untouched (uninhabited) stillness that would later form the early environmental debates over preservation. Meanwhile, the descendants of the mission's surviving families found themselves having to focus more on their own actual survival than on stewardship and caretaking the lands their ancestors had so long maintained.

—Martin Rizzo-Martínez and Mark Hylkema
(see About the Authors)

PREFACE

During one of my childhood visits to Big Basin in the late 1950s, we celebrated Jennie Bliss Jeter's ninety-eighth birthday. She delighted in teaching my brother and me how to "properly" feed the black-tail deer. The park had a transforming effect on our aunt—technically, as my great-grandfather's sister, she was our great-great-aunt, but we proudly called her our aunt Jennie, since she was the only one we had. She could seem austere in other settings but radiated with ease among the immense redwoods, as if she was among childhood friends.

Relishing this family gathering that would be her last, she recounted how Big Basin, California's first continuing state park, came to be. Aunt Jennie turned back the clock to her forty-first birthday: it was 1900, the year the campaign to save the imperiled redwood forest began. Actually, all I remembered about the story was the role of women, long before they had won the right to vote. Though Jennie downplayed her own role, my grandfather—her nephew and surrogate son—insisted that she was the force behind her husband, Will Jeter. His commitment to preserving "the great wonders of the world" began when he courted Jennie, who wanted public awareness of the fast-disappearing redwoods.

Many decades later and five thousand miles from Big Basin, I fed Sika deer at the beautiful park in Nara, Japan. What a thrill to encounter the famous wildlife with travelers from all over the world! The guide explained that in the Shinto religion, Sika deer are messengers of the gods, and they unexpectedly played that role for me. As I watched two deer become

Big Basin's natural defense—remote and mountainous terrain—protected the forest from nineteenth-century loggers. Boulder Creek, the closest town, is thirteen miles east. *Courtesy of Sourisseau Academy for State and Local History, San Jose State University.*

aggressive toward a child offering them official deer cookies, I flashed back to Big Basin. Of the many times friends and I had fed the black-tail deer at the park, we had experienced only their gentleness.

My disquieting realization at Nara—how much I'd taken the Santa Cruz Mountain redwoods for granted—haunted me. I'd even made an unkept promise to Aunt Jennie at age nine: "I'll never forget how the redwoods were saved." Yet I had no grasp of the complete story, only chunks of family history that no one had pieced together. On the trip home to Idaho from Japan, I made a detour to my birthplace of Santa Cruz to revisit Big Basin Redwoods State Park. What was the official version of the park's history? Once there, I took the docent tour, studied the brochure and perused each relevant book. Santa Cruz leaders—like William T. Jeter and Arthur A. Taylor—were not mentioned at all, even though the park is in our county. Moreover, women barely received a nod. How could my relatives have gotten it so wrong? Or did they?

I retired early from academia to pursue the Big Basin story full time. I loved my career as an education professor, but my mother's sudden passing fueled a sense of urgency. She had shared stories about Aunt Jennie, just as my grandfather and father had, but there was so much more I needed to know. Two relatives and one acquaintance of Jennie's still enjoyed good health in their eighties and lived not far from Santa Cruz. I wanted to spend time with each one while it was still possible. Their recollections proved indispensable given Jennie's intensely private nature. (See interviews in the bibliography.)

The decade-long study continued to reveal rich new layers about the men and women who never gave up, many of whom received little if any recognition for creating California's first permanent state park. They came together to do what no one else in the country had done before, not only because they loved the redwood forests but also because of their innate humanity.

What the research also uncovered was the equally moving part the forest played in its own survival. For centuries, it had existed in harmonious reciprocal relationship with the Indigenous peoples. After their removal, Big Basin resisted most exploitation for commercial gain. The most ancient redwoods did not defy just any lumberman eager to chop them down. In fact, the speculator—who acquired the land by a fraudulent scheme to deprive mixed-ancestry Dakota of their land rights—was altogether stymied by the remote topography. The Big Basin area that ultimately became the park, remained impenetrable. My immersion in the 140-year history that followed unveiled the valiant hero of this story: the primeval forest.

—Traci Bliss
(see About the Authors)

INTRODUCTION

While author Traci Bliss's journey getting this story into your hands is more than sixty years in the making, the exact timing of its coming onto the scene couldn't have been better planned. Important lessons from the historic campaign to save the Big Basin Forest not only resonate with social movements of today but will help produce a road map to reimagine a beloved park that's been recently leveled by a climate change–fueled disaster.

A Promise Made

The book you're holding is the result of a solemn promise made by a little girl more than six decades ago to her ninety-eight-year-old great-great-aunt, Jennie Bliss Jeter, on a family outing to Big Basin.

Jennie Bliss Jeter was one of the activists in the Big Basin preservation effort, and decades later, she'd play a pivotal role in the creation of Santa Cruz County Big Trees Park, which became Henry Cowell Redwoods State Park.

Traci Bliss was just a small child listening to her aunt Jennie's telling of the epic campaign to preserve the forest that would become Big Basin State Park: "You must never forget this story."

That admonition is the foundation of this book. Traci not only didn't forget, but the odyssey to tell this deeply personal story also eventually led her to leave a career in academia to start a years-long research project to track down other Big Basin campaign descendants, scour archives and libraries to unearth hidden stories and enlist a band of intrepid cohorts to find and provide never-before-published photos as part of the park's story.

ORIGIN STORIES

Parks have origin stories, most of which involve people in the community banding together to set aside a special place for protection and interpretation. These stories abound in Santa Cruz County State Parks history: the Adobe Coalition's fight to restore the Santa Cruz Mission Adobe and tell the story of the building used as housing for Native peoples at Mission Santa Cruz, the Operation Wilder campaign to save the historic dairy and surrounding land to create Wilder Ranch State Park and the epic fight to Save Lighthouse Field, to name a few.

Some of these origin stories are told more often than others, but in the case of Big Basin, a retelling of its creation has evolved into a mythology that frequently revolves around one great man or one heroic organization. Women who were key actors are sidelined, and scores of grassroots players are erased from history. In this book, their story is finally told and goes a long way toward busting those myths. In their place, the power of grassroots activism emerges, illuminating what a truly nonpartisan, sustained team effort can accomplish.

HIDDEN STORIES

Despite receiving pushback along the way for deviating from the mythology, Traci was steadfast in her commitment to tell a more complete story.

Starting with the Indigenous peoples of the Santa Cruz Mountains, whose ancestral homelands covered the eighteen thousand acres of the current state park, the foreword brings to light the important history of the community of people who called this area their home for thousands of years.

Also highlighted is a shocking, more modern story of Indigenous people halfway across the country whose misfortune at the hand of swindlers is also part of the Big Basin story.

A diversity of women's contributions is finally told. Jennie Bliss Jeter, Carrie Stevens Walter, Louise Coffin Jones and others each made a difference in her own way despite formidable societal constraints.

Further hidden stories are revealed, including how the Reverend George Jackson of the African Methodist Episcopal Zion Church in San Jose gave the first documented sermon in Big Basin and the son of Reverend Pon Fang was one of the very first children to camp in the park.

A Meaningful Place

Parks are deeply meaningful places for so many of us. They can be healing spaces for rest and renewal and connection with family, friends and our community. We've seen a surge in park visitation and connection throughout the COVID-19 pandemic. Sadly, the park that grew up in the twentieth century was laid waste by a fire in August 2020, causing heartbreaking devastation and disruption. Dozens of state parks staff suffered unimaginable losses due to the fire. Two of their compelling stories of resilient commitment are chronicled in the epilogue.

After the fire, the community swung into action to help. Donations poured into park partners such as Mountain Parks Foundation, the Sempervirens Fund, Save the Redwoods League and Friends of Santa Cruz State Parks (Friends). At Friends alone, 372 individuals and organizations from Vermont to Australia to British Columbia sent in donations large and small to help those most affected and to assist with park recovery. Many donations included heartfelt personal messages about what Big Basin means to them.

An Opportunity for the Future

While a profound tragedy, in so many ways, the catastrophe at Big Basin offers the community of park lovers a clean slate to reimagine the park in a way that makes sense for the next hundred years. How do we rebuild a new Big Basin in a way that protects the environment and restores recreational opportunities while ensuring equitable access? How can we create a resilient park during a time of climate crisis and also honor the intent of those who established it: "To be preserved in a state of nature"? One thing we can surely do is use this book to tell a more inclusive history of Big Basin. And we can write the next chapter of this storied park together in a way none of us could have imagined alone.

A Promise Kept

I'm so grateful to Traci Bliss. Grateful that she not only followed the threads of the story Jennie told her so many years ago but also that she's revealed the richness and complexity of the Big Basin campaign and shared it with us as an inspiration to continue to protect and enjoy this great redwood forest.

—Bonny Hawley
(see About the Authors)

GUIDE TO PHOTO ACKNOWLEDGEMENTS

Thanks to the exceptional archives at twenty institutions/ organizations, there is a robust visual record of the people, places and events that shaped Big Basin.

An institution's full courtesy line will appear the first time a photograph appears. As necessary, its subsequent photos will have a truncated courtesy line, shown below italicized.

The Bancroft Library, University of California, Berkeley

California State Library, Sacramento

Forest History Society Durham, North Carolina

Friends of Santa Cruz State Parks: *Friends*

History San Jose

Mill Valley Public Library, Lucretia Little History Room

Minnesota Historical Society, St. Paul

National Archives and Records Administration

Natural Resources and Public Health Library, University of California, Berkeley

San Francisco History Center/Public Library

San Jose Woman's Club

San Lorenzo Valley Museum

Santa Cruz Museum of Art & History: *Santa Cruz MAH*

Santa Cruz Public Library

Smith-Layton Archive, Sourisseau Academy for State and Local History, San Jose State University: *Sourisseau Academy SJSU*

Society of California Pioneers, San Francisco: *Society of California Pioneers*

Special Collections and Archives, Stanford University Libraries: *Special Collections Stanford*

Special Collections, Santa Clara University: *Special Collections SCU*

Special Collections, University Library, University of California Santa Cruz, Santa Cruz County Historical Photograph Collection: *Special Collections UCSC*

Statewide Museum Collections Center, California State Parks, Sacramento: *Museum Collections Center, State Parks.*

Sutter's Fort State Historic Park, Sacramento

Unless otherwise noted, historic photographs are the work of A.P. (Andrew Putnam) Hill
Unless otherwise noted, specific locations mentioned are in Santa Cruz City or County.

OWNERSHIP OF BIG BASIN IN THE NINETEENTH CENTURY

How did it happen that a trove of non-transferable land certificates, issued only to "half-breed" Dakota Sioux, were used by a white speculator to buy thousands of acres of Big Basin's virgin forest? And why did his exploitative scheme go awry?

Decades before any white men had laid eyes on the Big Basin landscape, seemingly unrelated events in Minnesota would profoundly shape its future. The 1825 Prairie du Chien Treaty set boundaries between the lands of the Dakota and seven other tribes in the region. This made it easier for government entities to negotiate to buy tribal lands. Five years later, a subsequent Prairie du Chien Treaty granted lands to the Dakota Sioux "half-breeds," the derogatory term used in those days for Native mixed-ancestry people. During negotiations, Chief Wabasha requested that a portion of the Dakota land, over 300,000 acres, be given to the tribes' "half-breed" members. (Today, this region includes Wabasha County in southeastern Minnesota, located on the western side of the Mississippi River.)[3]

When eager settlers descended on the highly desirable area twenty years later, a small group of "half-breed" Dakota Sioux responded. They had cultivated the area's "Half-breed" Tract at the Lake Pepin Minnesota Reservation for more than a decade and petitioned for their individual rights to be protected, that is, formalized. From there, a solution emerged to give them scrip (paper certificates), by which they could legally gain title to their land, specifically up to 480 acres on the "Half-breed" Tract.[4]

Yet it was another provision of the Act of July 17, 1854 that would impact Big Basin timberlands two thousand miles away in California. Suppose a "half-breed" or mixed-ancestry Dakota chose not to secure a land title at Lake Pepin. That individual was entitled to an allotment of up to 640 acres of unclaimed lands *anywhere* in the United States.[5] This wide-open promise to the "half-breeds" would help clear their tract for determined settlers who could claim the fertile land for themselves. Moreover, it enabled Minnesota-based land speculators to devise a nefarious scheme. "A loophole by which frauds have been perpetuated" was the characterization later offered by the *San Francisco Examiner*, owned and edited by William Randolph Hearst.[6]

William Randolph Hearst, an early supporter of saving Big Basin, used his *San Francisco Examiner* to promote the cause. Among big-city newspaper owners, his advocacy was the most consistent. *Courtesy of California State Library, Sacramento.*

The 1854 law clearly stated, "No transfer or conveyance of said certificate shall be valid," as did the certificates issued three years later. Nonetheless, two power of attorney forms attached to each piece of scrip, one to locate and one to sell, encouraged certificate holders to sell. Signing over their supposedly nontransferable rights, "half-breed" Dakota could receive cash for their land and avoid a cumbersome and alienating experience with the local land officials. Some settlers, eager to acquire the land for themselves, sought to intimidate scrip holders. "Two armed guards stood watch at the land office to keep scrip holders away."[7]

The intent of Congress in the 1854 law (that is, encouraging Native scrip holders to become landowners and assimilate into a more "American" way of life) was cunningly circumvented through the power of attorney forms. Those forms provided "the means to rob the real beneficiary."[8] Most of the scrip claimants did sell their land certificates and often for far less than their value. The certificate distributor who said, "The Half-breeds mostly got cats and dogs for their scrip,"[9] seemed especially accurate for describing those who decided to hold onto their certificates during the Civil War period. How could they possibly imagine the magnitude of the devastation awaiting them? In 1862, "American officials were months late in supplying the annuities and goods that had been guaranteed to the Dakota in previous treaties, leaving many Dakota people destitute and unable to feed themselves, ultimately leading to the U.S.–Dakota War. This was a costly and destructive war for both sides."[10]

Subsequently, noncombatant mixed-ancestry Dakota, consisting mostly of women, children and some older men who had not been convicted of crimes, were particularly vulnerable to exploitation. During the winter of 1862–63, many were imprisoned adjacent to Fort Snelling in St. Paul after a six-day, 150-mile journey from the Lower Sioux Agency. Franklin Steele, considered by many a hero in Minnesota history, had an exclusive government contract to provide food and supplies to the incarcerated Dakota. In other words, Steele was their lifeline amid the horrific conditions and overcrowding—concurrent with a statewide measles epidemic—at the makeshift concentration camp. The records show that by mid-March, forty-two people had died and by May, sixty more had succumbed.[11]

Half-breed Camp, a rare 1870 image, is the work of William H. Illingworth of St. Paul, a prolific photographer of the Midwest and West. *Courtesy of Minnesota Historical Society, St. Paul.*

It was there, where two hundred teepees were so close together that the desperate captives had no walking space between them, that the Minneapolis-based speculator William S. Chapman decided to make his big move. He instructed Steele, his business partner, "to get the deeds signed on these very valuable properties in a quiet way so as not to raise any talk among the Half-breeds. Some of my locations are so very valuable that I tremble when I think of the risk associated with delay."[12] Chapman clearly had confidence that Steele would find a considerable number of "half-breeds" among the 1,263 surviving Dakota[13] at the camp.

"Scrip had overwhelmed any real understanding of the land itself or the needs of the people who belonged to it,"[14] according to a prominent expert. The inside job enabled both speculators to amass a private hoard of Sioux scrip (the term used to describe the deeds). Steele would use his cache to help build his reputation and land holdings in Minnesota. But Chapman, originally from Ohio, apparently had no ties that bound him or his family to a state where they had lived for less than a decade. With his scrip treasure, he headed west in 1864, confident he would become the first owner of the extraordinary Big Basin timberlands and a prominent California land king.[15] Because of the loophole that allowed the scrip to be exchanged for government land any place it was available, the holder of the ill-gotten documents had almost unlimited opportunity.

Prior to the scandal at Fort Snelling, Chapman carefully studied government land allocations in Minnesota. He kept a calculating eye on any scrip issued in the 1850s and '60s, making him an expert at obtaining scrip of any kind and evidently by any means. But how did a midwesterner who had never seen a redwood know how "very valuable" Big Basin timber was?

William's brother, Isaac Chapman, helped ensure the cabal was not limited to Minnesota. He served as a deputy land surveyor in the Golden State, thoroughly acquainted with relevant surveys, documents and inquiries. This gave William Chapman a keen advantage over other speculators. In exchange for his collection of Sioux scrip, he wanted only the very best uncut timberland, and thanks to Isaac's position, he got it: thousands of acres in Big Basin, of which 2,320 were in Santa Cruz County.[16] (See Appendix A.)

William Chapman and his family settled north of Big Basin in San Francisco, a booming city where he used his expertise to become a dealer in land scrip while living for twenty years at the luxurious Palace Hotel. Despite his proximity, years of effort and the help of well-connected partners in San Mateo County, the densely wooded, mountainous area would not cooperate. Big Basin's topography made getting lumber to market next to impossible in

This very rare 1856 document is the actual scrip issued to "half-breed" Dakota Sioux Daniel Cratt, age one and a half. *Courtesy of National Archives and Records Administration.* *Transcribed excerpt from*:

SIOUX HALF-BREED RESERVE AT LAKE PEPIN.
(Not transferable or assignable.)

Issued in accordance with the provisions of the act of Congress, approved July 17, 1854, entitled "An act to authorize the President of the United States to cause to be surveyed the tract of land in the Territory of Minnesota belonging to the half-breeds or mixed bloods of the Dacotah or Sioux nation of the Indians, and for other purposes."

Therefore be it known, that this Certificate or Scrip issued by authority aforesaid, will entitle the said Daniel Cratt to locate, at the proper land office, the quantity of one hundred and sixty acres of land, as part of his four hundred and eighty acres claim, upon any of the lands within the said reservation that were not occupied on the 17th of July, 1854, by actual and bona fide settlers of the said half-breeds or mixed bloods, or such other persons as had at that date, or prior thereto, gone into said Territory, by authority of law, —or upon any other unoccupied lands subject to pre-emption or private sale, or upon any other unsurveyed lands not reserved by government, upon which they have respectively made improvements.

This Certificate or Scrip is not by law transferable, and any assignment or conveyance of the same is therefore void. *Transcription by Sally Iverson.*

the 1870s. How frustrating for a man accustomed to success by playing the angles[17] and getting others to buy into his scheme that the land he coveted for timber was impossible to tame.

Nearly twenty years after his machinations obtaining scrip from mixed-ancestry Dakota, Chapman finally gave up trying to profit from the many parcels of redwood forest he'd managed to consolidate. Although his predatory practices had contributed to a vast California land empire elsewhere—a half-million acres from Humboldt to Visalia—in 1881, he sold Big Basin. It is perhaps worth noting that despite all the wealth he accumulated during his forty years in the state, he died in 1906 "either broke or at the edge of bankruptcy."[18]

The new Big Basin owners were keen on putting a rail line from Boulder Creek through the mountains to the Pacific coast. Yet the forest averted another attempted onslaught when that plan also failed to materialize. In the mid-1880s, California's dominant monopoly, the Southern Pacific Railroad, stepped in. Would a railroad expansion now be inevitable or did the corporation's president, Leland Stanford, have something else in mind?

SETTING THE STAGE

Big Basin is located in the northernmost section of Santa Cruz County, with Santa Clara County and Stanford University as nearby neighbors. From each location, individuals—as diverse as they were dedicated—would compose the Big Basin movement. Serendipitous events throughout the last decades of the nineteenth century shaped their requisite roles.

STANFORD UNIVERSITY: VISION AND EXPERTISE

No tree in the United States could be made into more durable railroad ties then the coastal redwood. Santa Cruz County's San Lorenzo Valley, home to Big Basin, provided the ideal hub for harvesting the magnificent trees. The valley had lost more than a third of its original forest to railroad interests by the mid-1880s. At least two dozen local sawmills produced thirty-four million board feet annually. With Big Basin's uncut forest now in the hands of the Southern Pacific—called the "Octopus" because of the stranglehold it had on the state[19]—would anyone come to its rescue?

Ralph Smith, editor of the *San Mateo Times/Gazette*, spoke out in 1886, advocating for "a portion of the coast redwood forest…to be kept forever from destruction in any form."[20] Smith sent a letter to prominent Californians with an urgent wake-up call. He warned that a probable railroad expansion into Pescadero, at Big Basin's westernmost edge, would devastate the remaining forest.

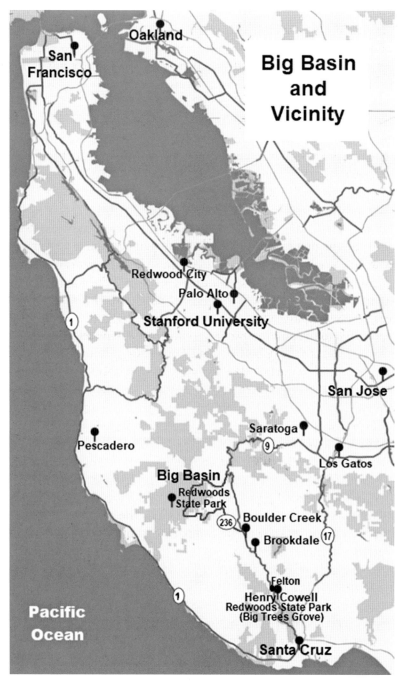

Individuals and organizations from Santa Cruz to San Francisco coalesced to create Big Basin State Park. This map is to show their relative proximity to the redwood forest. *Original design by Sally Iverson.*

A favorable response he received came from Senator Leland Stanford, one of the state's most powerful men and the wealthiest member of the United States Senate. Stanford had mentioned preserving stately forests from waste in his inaugural address as California's first Republican governor twenty-five years earlier.[21] Perhaps a promising alliance would have developed had Smith's life not come to a tragic end. In May 1887, an irate reader shot him on a street in Redwood City, north of what would later become Stanford University. Righteous and feisty A.A. Taylor, owner of the *Santa Cruz Surf* and Smith's friend, picked up the banner of his friend's cause to track almost every development relevant to Big Basin for more than three decades.

Also in May 1887, another death was memorialized when Senator Stanford laid the first cornerstone of Leland Stanford Junior University. He and wife Jane's only child, Leland DeWitt Jr., died three years earlier at age fifteen, prompting the couple's commitment to higher education in his honor. Watching the ceremony that day was a founding member of the board of trustees, twenty-eight-year-old Timothy Nolan Hopkins, whom Stanford had appointed to the position two years earlier. No single relationship would be more significant for Big Basin's storied progression of owners.

Timothy's mother, widowed at a young age, supported her two sons as a housekeeper in Sacramento. One of her clients was a childless couple, Mark and Mary Sherwood Hopkins, who informally adopted the promising young Timothy. He received the best possible education and looked forward to attending Harvard. At the time, Mark Hopkins's business partner and neighbor, Leland Stanford, also took a strong interest in the young boy. Both Stanford and Hopkins would amass considerable fortunes as owners of the Central Pacific Railroad—later the Southern Pacific—along with partners Colis Huntington and Charles Crocker. Under the ownership of the Big Four, as the men were known, the company became a monopoly, wielding undeterred power and influence.

When Mark Hopkins passed on in 1878, life changed for Timothy. Instead of attending Harvard as planned, he chose to become an apprentice at the railroad's headquarters, and a year later, Mary Hopkins officially adopted him. Stanford, as board president, no doubt looked out for the young man's best interests. Determined to learn all the inner workings of the family business, Timothy became one of Southern Pacific's directors and would also hold the position of company treasurer, just like his (adoptive) father. Given his attention to details, he might have learned the Big Basin chain of title holders. If so, to what degree might that information—that scrip

Above: United States senator Leland Stanford served as chairman of the Senate Committee on Public Buildings and Grounds (1887–93) when he announced his idea for Big Basin to become a grand park. *Courtesy of Special Collections, Stanford University Libraries.*

Opposite: *Evening Sunbeams* is an early example of A.P. Hill's two decades of unparalleled photo documentation of Big Basin. *Courtesy of Sourisseau Academy S.J.S.U.*

belonging to the mixed-ancestry Dakota had been used to purchase the land—have influenced his later actions?

Though Timothy conscientiously conducted business on his mother's behalf, he had no Southern Pacific assets of his own. Mark Hopkins did not leave a will. Did Mary's designer boyfriend from New York, twenty-two years her junior, know the entire estate belonged to her? Edward Searles proved to be a gallant suitor who indulged Mary's passion for building grand if not garish homes, much to Timothy's chagrin. Six months after the Stanford groundbreaking, Mary Hopkins married the New Yorker, and Timothy learned of the event via telegram.[22] Mr. Searles made haste taking power of attorney for Mary away from his stepson.

Did Hopkins's abrupt change in circumstances propel Stanford to bring a back burner issue to the fore? In August 1889, A.A. Taylor reported that the Southern Pacific Company would be converting the Big Basin region "into one of the greatest scenic places in the world."[23] Years later, the editor elaborated that Stanford wanted to annex it to the university as part of the

Above: Jane and Leland Stanford (*center*) laid the cornerstone for Stanford University on May 14, 1887. The environmental movement was initiated at Stanford thirteen years later with the vote to save Big Basin on May 1, 1900. (See page 61.) *Courtesy of Special Collections Stanford.*

Opposite: Hopkins Mansion, San Francisco. Timothy Hopkins and his mother, Mary, lived in their Nob Hill "palace" with Leland and Jane Stanford as next-door neighbors. *Courtesy of Special Collections Stanford.*

endowment. But in the late 1880s, other Southern Pacific decision-makers, most notably Colis Huntington—whose alleged resentment over Stanford's fame continued to simmer—considered a public park bad business.

When Southern Pacific owners convened in the spring of 1890, Searles had replaced Hopkins as a director and aligned himself with Huntington. With this newfound ally, Huntington, a man every member of the Hopkins family had distrusted, assumed the Southern Pacific's presidency. Stanford told Searles as much "because of the way Huntington had worked against him behind his back."[24]

Mary Hopkins Searles died the following year, explicitly leaving everything to Searles and nothing to Timothy: "Omission to provide in this will for my adopted son Timothy Hopkins is intentional and not occurring by accident or mistake."[25] When he sued the estate—worth $60 million—the tight-knit

San Francisco society circle took his side. The national press had a field day printing sensational details of the relationship between his mother and Mr. Searles, who confessed under oath to being partially motivated by Mary Hopkins's money. After losing in court, though not in public opinion, Hopkins implied he might divulge Southern Pacific's company secrets. That prompted months of out-of-court negotiations. All hope for Big Basin could have been lost had Leland Stanford not helped ensure that Hopkins, his protégé, had the best possible legal team behind him.

In the 1892 settlement, Timothy Hopkins received what he wanted: forty thousand acres of redwoods and controlling interests in the Loma Prieta and Pescadero lumber companies, which included nearly all of the prime Big Basin acreage. He now held the largest amount of uncut timber in the region. In a *Surf* editorial, Taylor extended hearty congratulations to "the liberal minded and progressive young man."[26] The editor made clear that if the land titles had stayed with Edward Searles, the Southern Pacific would have continued its control and opposition to any park.

All the while, Leland Stanford supported his visionary president, David Starr Jordan, in creating a world-class university. Jordan, a renowned biologist specializing in ichthyology, traveled the country to handpick each faculty member. He tapped his close friend, Cornell professor William Dudley, to be the chair of Stanford University's systemic botany department. The two men were undergraduate roommates at Cornell, and both were enthralled by the tallest trees in the world: coastal redwoods officially known as *Sequoia sempervirens* (ever-green or ever-living).

Timothy Hopkins married his mother's niece, Mary Kellogg Crittenden, in 1892. She joined him in his wide-ranging efforts to support Stanford University. *Courtesy of Special Collections Stanford.*

Dudley had barely settled in at Stanford in 1892 when he joined Jordan at the Sierra Club, which the president had helped to found. The organization proved important to Big Basin's creation thanks to the wide-reaching influence of its members: "Almost 1/3 of the club's 182 charter members were academics, many in the natural sciences from the new University of California, Stanford University, Mills College in Oakland and the California Academy of Sciences in San Francisco. Only five were women; the rest of them were almost all businessmen and lawyers working in San Francisco's financial district…where the club established its headquarters."[27]

With the door finally closed on family drama, Hopkins refocused his energy on being a Stanford trustee. He and his wife, Mary, had a summer home adjacent to the university in Menlo Park where they fostered a close relationship with Jordan. The president advocated for preservation against greedy speculators and practiced what he preached. For the university's entire first class, he led a field trip to the Santa Cruz Mountain redwoods.

A month later, in June 1893, Leland Stanford died with his university positioned to possibly make a reality of the vision: public ownership of the redwoods. Hopkins, traveling in Europe with Mary, telegraphed for his nursery to donate all the floral arrangements to honor his mentor, and he returned in time to stand at Jane Stanford's side for the reading

In 1890, the Maddock family, Irish immigrants with eight children, got a legitimate title to a 160-acre section in Big Basin. Their years of productive homesteading included building this cabin out of a single redwood. *Courtesy of Deborah Maddock Elston.*

San Lorenzo River, Big Trees Grove, Felton, 1892. Professor William R. Dudley (*left*) with Stanford students and staff on an outing to the old-growth redwoods. *Courtesy of Special Collections Stanford.*

This is the type of trail made by the Stanford Outing Club in the 1890s when most of Big Basin belonged to Stanford trustee Timothy Hopkins. *Courtesy of Special Collections, University of California Santa Cruz Library, Santa Cruz County Historical Photograph Collection.*

Botany professor Dudley provided essential data for the Big Basin campaign. His proactive stewardship included serving on the first California Redwood Park Commission. *Courtesy of Special Collections Stanford.*

of Leland's will. By all accounts, Hopkins considered the couple family and would have endeavored to bring Leland's vision for Big Basin to fruition.

In 1897, the tenth anniversary of the university's founding, Hopkins received special accolades for his munificence. Having missed out on college himself, his philanthropy focused on expanding students' learning opportunities such as the Hopkins Marine Laboratory on the Monterey Bay and an expanded library. When Dudley created the Stanford Outing Club, Hopkins provided the necessary access to Big Basin, where students assisted the professor with surveying and making trails. No records exist of any other group being given that privilege.

As Dudley became the world's leading expert on the botany and topography of Big Basin,[28] he agreed to serve as the editor of the Sierra Club's bulletin, an ideal platform to promote preservation. The dedicated group, under John Muir's leadership, had already succeeded in preserving the Sierra's giant sequoias. In a paper given at the San Francisco–based club, Dudley advocated for "a strong effort to secure from private owners some basin…such as the Big Basin to serve as a natural park and an illustration to future generations of the grandeur of the primeval coast range forest." The *San Francisco Call* and *San Jose Evening News* reprinted his remarks, ensuring the professor's vision went well beyond club members.[29]

SANTA CRUZ COUNTY: STEWARDS AND COMMUNITY INVOLVEMENT

Jennie Bliss, born in December 1859, grew up on a farm outside Chicago where her father, Moses, a staunch abolitionist, provided support to the Underground Railroad.[30] When she was eighteen, he pursued a new mission for his family: helping to spread northern Methodist values in the sparsely populated West.

Victorian norms required women to be demure, paragons of domestic virtue and without political opinions of their own. Jennie met none of those criteria. Rather, she defied convention by riding astride, being an accomplished golfer and never learning to cook. Additionally, for Jennie, who had planned to attend the Chicago Art Institute, leaving the maple forests she cherished for the roughhewen West felt like a step backward.

Imagine the contrast between the budding arts culture of Chicago and the wood-planked sidewalks of small-town Santa Cruz with fewer than four

Above: The Sherman Tree at Big Trees Grove—today Henry Cowell Redwoods State Park—became Jennie Bliss Jeter's favorite redwood to paint due to its abundance of burls. *Public domain.*

Opposite: Jennie Bliss, at Moses Bliss home, 515 Highland Avenue, 1883, before her marriage to William Jeter. Her deep conviction was "everyone deserves free and easy access to the ancient redwoods." *Courtesy of Santa Cruz Museum of Art & History.*

thousand residents. But soon enough, Jennie discovered a new forest with trees three times as tall as midwestern maples. On horseback, she could make it from her home to the Big Trees Grove in Felton in less than two hours. From her artist's point of view, the redwoods embodied the ideal of community—a place where all belonged in supportive relationship. (As an example, the trees' shallow root systems tightly intertwine, providing stability during intense winds.) Her weekly trips to the Grove revealed that the ancient trees, some nearly two thousand years old, had to be preserved—and not just on canvas. Only one other area of uncut old-growth forest remained in the San Lorenzo Valley—the lush Big Basin wilderness, twenty-five miles away. The full day's journey from Santa Cruz required train changes and then at least a dozen miles on horseback or in a horse-drawn buggy over a road replete with potholes.

Given her Methodist values of service to humanity, she felt compelled to show the community how decades of logging had defaced the Santa Cruz Mountains. But how? Organizing a group of five close women friends in 1884, she led them on a six-mile trek through the arduous terrain from

41

Santa Cruz to Big Trees Grove, owned by the preservationist-minded Welch family and where the Rose Club had its annual picnic. Determined to make a grand entrance at the event, Jennie was certain the press would follow her bloomer-clad adventurers. They were cleverly drawing attention to the forest devastation en route to a fashionable luncheon.

But the media chose not to mention the denuded forest when the local economy depended on redwood logging. Instead, the reporter focused on the "pedestriennes" unsustainable derring-do: "They did not care to walk back to this city, and were only too delighted to ride on the train homeward."[31] But not so for headstrong Jennie, who completed the round-trip journey on foot. Though her public awareness effort flopped, she did gain the rapt attention of a most eligible suitor.

Local lawyer William T. Jeter, attending the Rose Club's luncheon, admired her gumption. The aspiring politician assured Jennie he could help with redwood preservation throughout Santa Cruz County. In 1884, Jeter became the first Democrat to be elected Santa Cruz County district attorney, and soon after, the couple married. Twelve years later, he would

Teams of oxen were well suited for hauling huge redwood logs. *Author's Collection.*

42

be sworn in as California's lieutenant governor—a position, unbeknownst to him, that laid essential groundwork for the Big Basin crusade.

As a husband-and-wife team, Jennie expected they would initiate a movement to save the mountain redwoods, but Jeter's commitments as DA and as a city councilman left little time for the seemingly non-urgent issue. However, newspaperman A.A. Taylor did consider the trees a pressing concern and hired a "traveling reporter" for the *Surf*. Captain Fredrick Clarke produced detailed descriptions and photos of the flora, fauna, creeks and ridges within Big Basin. When he escorted Taylor on a camping trip, the editor became even more convinced that the area had to be preserved "as a typical California forest for all time to come"[32] and expected other newspaper editors in his network to join in.[33]

In 1892, Jeter, with Taylor's strong support for his progressive vision and agenda, achieved another milestone for local Democrats. He became the first one to be elected mayor of Santa Cruz. Both men were in their early forties, the former six foot six and the latter barely five feet, if that. Both shared tough-minded support for the common man. Their styles, however, were opposite: Jeter, always the gentleman with a steel-trap mind, and Taylor, the ardent and restless provocateur. Their political allegiance solidified around grand ideas for Santa Cruz County, most notably its extensive mountain range and remaining forests.

On an excursion to Pescadero, Will (as he was known to family and friends) showed Jennie his hopes for a Skyline Highway that would one day connect all the redwood groves between Santa Cruz and San Francisco. But a day filled with promise ended with a life-changing tragedy. On their way home, an out-of-control milk wagon driver careened into their buggy, hitting Jennie in the stomach with the rail of the wagon.[34] Jeter made sure that local reporting did not mention that she was pregnant and lost their child. How would Jennie, now thirty-two, fill the void of never being a mother? She found renewed purpose dedicating herself to making the redwoods forever accessible, most especially for families.

As treasurer, Jennie energized fellow members of the Santa Cruz Improvement Society with her idea to raise funds for resurfacing Big Trees Road (today's Highway 9). The society more than met its financial goal, but what captured a reporter's attention was the mix of backgrounds among the event's three hundred attendees. They came from "the church, the societies, the dancing set, the fraternal organizations; from the old, the young and middle-aged."[35] He accurately captured what Jennie hoped to cultivate: an inclusive common cause of improved access to the trees.

Above: Mill near Bear Creek, 1880s. When traveling by horseback in the Santa Cruz Mountain range, one would have likely encountered a sawmill in operation. *Courtesy of the Santa Cruz MAH.*

Left: William T. Jeter left school after eighth grade to support his widowed mother and siblings. He served the city of Santa Cruz as a councilman and mayor, the county as district attorney and the state as lieutenant governor. For nearly four decades he was Santa Cruz County Bank president. *Courtesy of Santa Cruz MAH.*

Jeter, while mayor, accepted the presidency of the Santa Cruz County First National Bank (eventually called the County Bank), a position he would hold for the rest of his long life. It was the era in California when the banker knew his borrower "and all about him, his resources, manner in which he conducted his business and the amount of money he owed."[36] Fortuitously, one of his first clients in 1893 was Henry Middleton of Boulder Creek, a close friend from the Democratic Party. Though he had spent a decade building up his timber interests, valley residents knew him best for developing the lumber town of Boulder Creek. Like Jeter, he had no children of his own

The *San Francisco Call* published this etching to celebrate William Jeter's rebuilt County Bank in 1895, after a fire devastated downtown Santa Cruz the previous year. *Courtesy of Randall Brown Collection.*

and became a father figure for the town. In addition to the water company, he co-owned the largest dry goods store in the area and built a sixteen-room hotel at the crossroads to the future park. The two structures would serve as a type of base camp for the Big Basin excursions—field trips designed to create enthusiasm for the campaign.

At the end of Jeter's term as mayor, disaster struck Santa Cruz. On the night of April 14, 1894, major sections of the downtown went up in flames. As buildings crumbled, Jeter helped to prevent any lives from being lost while his bank building burned to the ground.[37] With record speed, he purchased a new bank location at the very center of town. Opening in less than a year, the bank—with a breathtaking Renaissance design—achieved its objective.[38] It rallied the community even as the nation suffered a severe economic downturn. Although Jeter was adept at self-effacing modesty, his behind-the-scenes leadership propelled the city's rebirth and garnered attention well beyond Santa Cruz.

While locals were consumed with rebuilding, a Big Basin development came and went virtually unnoticed. *Surf* editor Taylor picked up on the story, oddly titled "Hot Stuff," but included none of his usual analysis.[39] Lucy Frasier Abraham, a mixed-ancestry Dakota, was in her twenties when William S. Chapman scoured the Fort Snelling internment camp for scrip holders. Recently, one of the certificates bearing the name of Lucy Frasier had turned up in an attempted sale by Chapman. But Lucy, in a sworn affidavit, said she never met the man nor signed any certificate over to him in 1861—the date on the power of attorney. Had Chapman forged documents during the year prior to the Dakota "half-breeds" being conveniently incarcerated in one place? Just two weeks after filing her complaint in September 1894, Lucy Frasier Abraham—not Chapman—received a $1,000 check from the buyer of a Big Basin section of land. A local judge had taken seriously a United States government document—that is, the scrip that specified *non-transferable*. At least one mixed-ancestry Dakota received justice, albeit decades after the scheme at Fort Snelling.

THE POWER OF POLITICAL ACCOMPLISHMENT

In October 1895, Governor James Budd appointed Jeter—his former unsuccessful running mate—as lieutenant governor when the man elected to the office suddenly died. Budd's health challenges—some critics claimed alcoholism—required Jeter to frequently serve as governor, and many Santa Cruzans insisted on using the title thereafter. Yet it was his role presiding over the Senate, revamping the rules and procedures, that solidified his "man of the people" reputation. Senators honored Jeter in a special ceremony as a "gentleman of the old school"; his trustworthiness across party lines would be required when Big Basin needed it the most.

While lieutenant governor, he continued his habit of showing off Santa Cruz's "great wonders of the world." Such events kept locals interested in their remarkable trees, if not in person, then through the news coverage of the day. For example, years earlier, Jeter orchestrated the first presidential visit to Big Trees Grove.[40] From his vantage holding a statewide office, he invited national organizations—Woodcutters, Apple Growers and others—often with as many as one thousand members attending.

In 1897, his well-meaning invitation to the National Christian Endeavor Society became a shocking embarrassment for Santa Cruz. When hundreds

White-haired President Benjamin Harrison, a champion for forests, visited Santa Cruz in 1892. At Big Trees Grove, he quietly communed with the redwoods, refusing a single photograph. *Courtesy of Santa Cruz MAH.*

Irascible Stanly Welch avoided any photographs of himself at his family's Big Trees Grove in Felton, but he relished being photographed at the Calaveras Big Trees South Grove. *Author's Collection.*

of devout women arrived at the Grove in Felton, they were instantly in awe of the trees but disgusted by the admission fee. With the price of redwood lumber on the rise, Stanly Welch, who served as the family's proprietor at Big Trees, could cash in as a preservationist. Anyone entering the Grove through his fourteen-foot-high fence was required to pay twenty-five cents, an increase of fifteen cents overnight. Jennie, who had promoted the event, was understandably livid; unless you were a family of means, you couldn't afford to be among the trees and there was no alternative. In a scathing piece, Taylor concurred, calling the event "the big tree swindle" and, along with the *San Jose Herald*, suggested Big Basin be made into a state "pleasure ground."[41]

At the end of his term in Sacramento in 1898, Jeter collapsed from exhaustion.[42] During his hush-hush recovery, Jennie entreated him just to focus on preservation. The accelerated devastation of Santa Cruz Mountain redwoods had become an unquestionably urgent issue. As the national economy recovered, timber cutting in the San Lorenzo Valley had roared back.

SANTA CLARA COUNTY ACTIVISTS: JOURNALISTS AND JESUITS

Victorian-era women's groups such as the Daughters of the American Revolution, Native Daughters of the Golden West, the Woman's Christian Temperance Union and the suffragists, to name a few, had their own important agendas. At the San Jose Women's Club (SJWC), however, members prided themselves on putting aside conflicting allegiances for the greater good. The club, an incubator for activists, was ideally positioned for a leadership role in saving Big Basin.

Originally from Massachusetts, Catherine Brown Smith founded and organized the San Jose Women's Club and also served as president, though unofficially, during the initial years. Smith, an ardent feminist, insisted on being known by her second husband's name: Mrs. E.O. Smith. Her first husband died while serving in the Union army, leaving her to raise two young children alone until she met Edward Owen Smith in the late 1860s. Widowed for a second time in 1892, she dedicated herself to reform activities in San Jose and throughout California. As vice president of the Pacific Coast Women's Press Association (PCWPA), she championed the importance of women's voices being heard and presented an influential paper to members in 1895. In "Sex Lines in Literature," she made the case that world literature "had been mainly masculine, the absence of women… being due to her subservient position in all departments of life."[43]

As vice president of the California Women's Suffrage Association, the charismatic Smith was in high demand in the role of featured speaker. When the 1896 campaign to pass a state suffrage amendment failed, she continued her commitment, maintaining a vast network of supporters from throughout California. But it was through the PCWPA that she came to know another prominent writer who eschewed the suffrage movement while wholeheartedly embracing preservation.

The daughter of a midwestern minister, Carrie Stevens Walter enjoyed a career as a teacher at the Eagle School in the Berryessa district of San Jose. By the mid-1880s, she had established herself as a well-respected writer whose articles and poems found a receptive audience in the *Overland Monthly*. Simultaneously, she used every available avenue—advertisements, pamphlets and letters to the editor—to promote Northern California, especially Santa Clara County, where she had spent her teenage years. Her travel magazine—the *Santa Clara*—extolled the virtues of San Jose and its surroundings. During the height of her writing career, she and her husband lived separately, and one rumor mill said he had deserted his wife and children for the gold fields.

Focusing her noteworthy talent on issues such as historic preservation, she earned the respect of prominent newspapermen from Santa Cruz to Sacramento. It was no small feat being the only woman publisher in a clubby world of men. With ever-expanding name recognition, she became a prominent voice in the San Jose Women's Club, of which she was a charter member. As soon as the Big Basin campaign got underway, the visionary SJWC president, Mrs. Stephen A. Jones, formerly Louise Coffin, became her regular companion in their common cause.

Carrie Stevens Walter joined ten other women as a founding member of the San Jose Woman's Club in 1894. In 1900, two hundred members made Big Basin a club priority. *Public domain.*

Louise grew up in a family of devoted abolitionists in Indiana. In 1868, during Reconstruction, the eighteen-year-old

Quaker activist headed to Little Rock, Arkansas, where the Society of Friends hired her and another woman to teach in a school for Black children. Yet for their commitment, "the two young women teachers were ostracized from the society of the white people."[44]

In 1872, she taught school near San Gregorio in San Mateo County adjacent to the Big Basin Forest. Louise explored the area on horseback at a time when very few had firsthand experience of the area. Captivated by the redwoods' unique beauty, she wrote a nature article for an Indiana newspaper and included her delightful discovery of a banana slug.[45] By 1875, after teaching in another school, she was back in Indiana playing a major role in the writing of her uncle's autobiography. *The Reminisces of Levi Coffin* documented his fearless and shrewd support of thousands of fugitive slaves, earning him the unofficial name of "President of the Underground Railroad."

Throughout her twenties, Louise was motivated by religious convictions and finding good stories to write, which included covering the Centennial Exposition in Philadelphia. She was twenty-six in 1876, beyond the age at which society assigned the derogatory term "old maid" to an unmarried woman. But that soon changed when she married an equally committed member of the Society of Friends, Professor Stephen Jones. During his term as the president of the University of Nevada, Louise befriended the Paiute and Washoe tribes, continuing her early commitment to helping those discriminated against.

When the family settled in San Jose in 1894, contributing to the community became her all-absorbing focus. Just as Jones's early articles for *Good Housekeeping* and *Lippincott's* made distant forest and mountain habitats come alive for her readers, she inspired SJWC members with photographs of the stunning natural landscapes of Calaveras and Yellowstone. Widely traveled, Louise was a leader for the quiet transformation occurring in women across the country. Members of garden clubs—once satisfied to focus on their individual domains—intentionally expanded their horizons to the natural world. "Moral guardians of nature" aptly described an emerging new identity to which women aspired at the close of the nineteenth century.[46]

Though not a member of the SJWC, Josephine Clifford McCrackin maintained a close connection with Catherine Brown Smith and Carrie Stevens Walter—as all three were original members of the Pacific Coast Women's Press Association. Josephine spent her childhood in the Black Forest region of Germany before her family immigrated to St. Louis, Missouri, where she received a rigorous Catholic education. Later, having

Louise Coffin Jones, adventuresome and independent during the Victorian era, reflected her Quaker upbringing. The American Society of Friends emphasized equality between men and women. *Courtesy of Jones Family Collection.*

endured a harrowing escape from her abusive first husband, she led a bohemian life in San Francisco. In middle age, she and her second husband managed their Monte Paraiso vineyard off Summit Road between Santa Cruz and San Jose.

Jackson McCrackin supported Josephine's endeavors as a horticulturalist in the small community of German American winemakers but not her talent as a writer. Her "forced" retirement from journalism ended, however, when Monte Paraiso's many acres of redwood grove went up in flames in 1899.

Josephine wanted her story told and contacted a San Jose artist friend, A.P. Hill, to provide photographs of the smoldering ruins of her hilltop home. For illustrating the beauty of what had been lost, Hill thought photos from Big Trees Grove would be ideal.[47] Alas, when proprietor Stanly Welch caught him taking unauthorized pictures on his land, he demanded the negatives. A furious Hill made a vow to himself that he would start a campaign. Consistent with his take-action style, Hill immediately enlisted the San Jose Board of Trade (SJBOT) and the SJWC, where his wife, Florence, was a member, to help promote his cause.

Both organizations sent letters to the Santa Cruz Board of Trade (SCBOT) proposing that Big Trees Grove become a park owned by the public. (By

(*Left to right*): Jackson McCrackin, Ambrose Bierce, Josephine McCrackin. Bierce, a featured writer for the *San Francisco Examiner* and close friend of Josephine's, was staying at the ranch when her world turned to ashes in 1899. *Courtesy of Special Collections Stanford.*

1908, the Board of Trade would become the Santa Cruz Chamber of Commerce.)

In addition to his artistic talent, Hill excelled at networking among various Santa Clara County organizations. During the campaign, he gave them vital updates to which he was privy. Early on, he involved his alma mater, the Jesuit-run Santa Clara College. The institution provided the movement with something no other organization could: the uncommon diligence of its highly regarded president, Father Robert Kenna, and his network of priests and committed Catholic parishioners throughout the Bay Area and beyond.

Back in Santa Cruz, the SCBOT, which included Jennie Jeter's brother Frank Bliss, had received the letters from San Jose but had no interest in pursuing a park at Big Trees Grove. A popular Victorian tourist Mecca—

Florence Watkins Hill, from a family of independent-thinking women, married artist A.P. Hill (*Left to right*): Mabel Hill, Laura Watkins, Lawrence Hyde, Florence Watkins Hill and Andrew P. Hill Jr., circa 1888. *Courtesy of Sourisseau Academy S.J.S.U.*

consisting of just forty acres of old-growth trees—could hardly ignite a statewide movement.[48] It was not in danger of being logged, and the Welch siblings, already preserving it, showed no eagerness to sell. But Hill had opened the door for action. The SCBOT unanimously supported a motion by Dr. Charles Andersen, a well-respected botanist: "A large park taking in the Big Basin…should be immediately preserved."[49] For the first time in California's history, an organization specifically committed to saving Big Basin.

Events moved quickly in March 1900. On the seventh, *Santa Cruz Sentinel* owner Duncan McPherson published a letter from Josephine titled "Save the Trees," in which she eloquently urged the people of California to lobby their legislators. Her rousing words focused on Welch's mercenary action of charging an entrance fee "as utterly un-American" and called for the Grove to be made public. She did not mention Big Basin or include her signature, an omission Josephine regretted later on. Reflecting the culture of the time, she

Above: Father Kenna, president of Santa Clara College, gathered with a group of Jesuit priests in Big Basin well before the official start of the movement. *Courtesy of Special Collections SCU.*

Left: Landscape artist and photographer A.P. Hill attended Santa Clara College for a year, where he made lifelong connections essential to the Big Basin movement. *Courtesy of Sourisseau Academy SJSU.*

worried that if folks saw a woman's name it would diminish the importance of her plea. Instead, she signed her work "An Old Californian."[50]

Significantly, the two boards of trade—San Jose and Santa Cruz—now had a joint cause. The latter group invited William Jeter to represent them based on his track record in the county and in Sacramento. But what exactly was the path forward? It would become clear with two unplanned events: First, a very public win for women preservationists, and second, a closed-door deal between the men who owned Big Basin.

A NEW ERA BEGINS

At the start of the twentieth century, Californians wrote a bold new chapter in their history. Well-connected women used their associations on Capitol Hill to score a decisive win for forest preservation, providing momentum for the long-awaited Big Basin crusade.

Two types of redwoods naturally occur in California: the giant sequoia found on the western slope of the Sierra Nevada, the world's largest living trees (circumference-wise), and the coast redwood (*Sequoia sempervirens*), the world's tallest. The giant sequoias of Calaveras County had attracted thousands of visitors annually since the early 1850s. Fascinated sightseers called them "Tree Giants." When word leaked out in 1900 that the cherished Grove would likely be replaced with a sawmill operation, concerned citizens vehemently protested.

The California Club of San Francisco, composed of socially prominent women, took charge. Laura Lovell White, club founder and wife of a powerful banker, involved her close friend Phoebe Apperson Hearst. An extraordinarily wealthy, politically accomplished widow, Hearst was perhaps the most well-known woman in the state. The first to serve on University of California Board of Regents, she initiated and funded the all-female dormitory on campus, one of many endeavors for the school.[51] When Mrs. Hearst agreed to help lobby Congress to save Calaveras, people took note. Her son, William Randolph Hearst, editorialized for the cause in his paper: "Who will save from destruction the magnificent *Sequoia gigantea* forest of California?"[52]

The women of San Francisco's California Club were lauded for saving the Calaveras Big Trees Grove in 1900. This tree, named Empire State, may be the North Grove's largest giant sequoia. *Author's Collection.*

To a conference of fruit growers convened at Stanford, botanist William Dudley talked up the California Club's efforts, calling preservation the civic duty of right-minded citizens. The *San Jose Herald*—listing the many organizations involved—saluted its own SJWC for a "most earnest protest against this work of wanton devastation and vandalism."[53]

By mid-March 1900, Congress passed a resolution preventing what had become the state's longest-running tourist attraction from falling victim to the axe. In short, saving Calaveras Big Trees—officially designated a national forest in 1909 and finally a state park in 1931—showed how effectively women mobilized.[54] A.A. Taylor, praising the California Club's initiative, used the victory to remind Santa Cruzans that a park in Big Basin should be next. "Perhaps there is work here and now for women to do."[55]

As he and others in the media focused on the Calaveras triumph, Jeter—far from the public's view—facilitated a strategic rapprochement between two antagonistic lumber companies. Since gaining title to the prime sections of Big Basin, Timothy Hopkins had left the land untouched and allowed access to only Professor Dudley for his Stanford Outing Club. It appeared Hopkins had made Leland Stanford's dream of a public park his own but took no action in that direction until 1898, when he blocked his neighbor's logging efforts.

The neighbor happened to be Jeter's client and close friend Henry Middleton. The unofficial mayor of Boulder Creek enjoyed a lucrative contract to provide lumber for railroad ties to the Southern Pacific from his own section of Big Basin. However, to reach the company's sawmill, his lumbermen needed to go by way of Hopkins's road. Starting in 1898, they no longer had access: a heavy barbed wire fence blocked the thoroughfare.[56]

Through a business deal unrelated to Big Basin, Hopkins interacted with Jeter for the first time in March 1900; his initial impressions must have been positive. Would a deal with Henry Middleton be possible? Jeter believed so and created an opportunity for them to meet. Soon after, the two landowners inspected their Big Basin holdings together.[57]

Born into a highly successful lumber family in Guerneville, how much soul-searching would someone like Henry Middleton do in April 1900? After all, the value of Big Basin lumber would soar as the economy continued to recover from the severe downturn. On the other hand, his beloved town of Boulder Creek would benefit from tourism related to a public park. Which path would it be? Hopkins no doubt made the pitch that through a merger with him, Middleton could meet his obligations to provide railroad ties using lumber from one of Hopkins's other lumber locations.

In 1900, lumberman Henry Middleton's behind-the-scenes decision to partner with preservation-minded timber owner Timothy Hopkins made a public park possible. *Courtesy of Special Collections UCSC.*

On April 24, 1900, Hopkins's and Middleton's combined timber holdings officially became the **Big Basin Lumber Company**, an entity willing to sell the land at a fair price for the cause of preservation.[58] Revered by valley residents and by the regional lumber industry, Middleton became the voice of the new company. Hopkins, with the lion's share of the land, assumed the role of silent partner.

Jeter immediately turned to creating a core coalition. He could count on his own preexisting networks of policy makers and bankers, but he wanted academic expertise strongly represented. With no firsthand experience in higher education, he had developed confidence in the professors he had

"Animal Tree"
Big Basin, Calif.

Above: May 1, 1900, was a milestone in environmental history. Sixteen individuals gathered at Stanford University to officially launch the Big Basin campaign. (*Left to right*): J.H. Singer, University of California, Berkeley; David Starr Jordan, Stanford; William R. Dudley, Stanford; Frederick W. Billing, Santa Cruz Board of Trade SCBOT; J.M. Stillman, Stanford; J.Q. Packard (SCBOT); Lieutenant Governor William T. Jeter SCBOT; Judge John E. Richards, San Jose; Carrie S. Walter, San Jose Woman's Club; James McNaughton, San Jose Normal School; Charles B. Wing, Stanford; John J. Montgomery, Santa Clara College; R.L. Green, Stanford. Not pictured: Father Robert E. Kenna, Santa Clara College, Josephine McCrackin, Pacific Coast Women's Press Association, and Andrew P. Hill, the photographer. *Courtesy of Santa Cruz MAH.*

Opposite: At the turn of the century, few Californians had firsthand experience of Big Basin's sublime landscape and trees such as this one. Among the many redwood burls visitors saw animal shapes and aptly named it the Animal Tree. *Courtesy of Frank Perry Collection.*

come to know while serving as an ex-officio member of the University of California Board of Regents while lieutenant governor.

Surely Hopkins, his new ally, helped orchestrate the movement's official launch at Stanford, just one week after the creation of Big Basin Lumber Company. Sixteen prominent men and women gathered at the university where the Committee to Save the Redwoods gave birth to a very focused crusade. Well over half of those involved were college presidents and faculty members from the botany, chemistry, engineering and math departments at Stanford, Berkeley, San Jose Normal School and Santa Clara College. Other members included Carrie Walter representing the SJWC, Josephine McCrackin the PCWPA and three businessmen from the SCBOT.[59]

Bloom's Mill was located near the edge of Big Basin. I.T. Bloom was most eager to expand his lumbering into the untouched areas of the forest. *Courtesy of History San Jose.*

As the group's elected president, Jeter relied on Dudley's maps and firsthand knowledge of Big Basin to give a data-driven presentation of the big picture. According to the *San Jose Mercury*:

> *Mr. Jeter was well supplied with facts and figures. He made an extensive and very interesting report, showing maps of the tract and explaining that they…were in a position to assure the committee that all the land could be acquired from the owners at less than its actual worth and at a comparatively small cost. He also explained the danger which immediately threatened this virgin forest, showing that there were a number of large mills around the borders of the basin, which this year and next would penetrate the very heart of the Big Basin and denude it of timber.*[60]

The committee unanimously voted to save the Big Basin. Jeter, with Dudley as secretary, would develop the political strategy; Santa Cruzans John F. Coope and John C. Packard, Jeter's business associates, would build strategic alliances through immersive experiences at Big Basin. Their selective invitations to a few organizations offered a weeklong excursion into the heart of the forest to gather data.[61] Who would join them for an adventuresome, all-expenses paid field trip? SJWC selected Carrie Walter and club president Louise Jones to attend; SJBOT sent photographer A.P. Hill to capture the scenic beauty. The Fish and Game Protective Association assigned outdoorsmen W.W. Richards and Roley Kooser, and the San Francisco Board of Supervisors sent one of its own, attorney Charles Reed.

BUILDING A COMMITTED COALITION

Henry Middleton welcomed the SCBOT's excursion party of six men and two women at the Boulder Creek depot just two weeks after the launch at Stanford. Like a proud father, he relished the role of Big Basin's gracious proprietor—one he would continue in for several years. In addition to the best camping gear from his dry goods store, Middleton provided the adventurers with unexpected amenities. Describing the delicious "camp" dinner that evening, Carrie Walter noted, "Even enthusiasts cannot live on scenery alone."[62]

The group's guide, on the very first day, led them to a twenty-three-hundred-foot ridge at the intersection of Waddell, Pescadero and Butano Creeks, whence they had "a magnificent view of the Big Basin." Whether trout fishing in the San Lorenzo River or moving through one cluster of trees to the next, the explorers were enthralled with the grandeur of what to them represented an untouched wilderness.

Carrie vividly shared their experience with the public: "We crossed rushing streams, clear as crystal—streams that set certain fishermen of our party wild with delight. Wherever we went, above us, towered the great redwoods, the grand 'old guard' of the water sources.…Many men are awakening to the beauty of these forest aisles. The first Gothic temple, they say was formed by forest trees. God grant that they be also the last!"[63]

Thoroughly infused with the aura of Big Basin, a reverential mood permeated the group—no one needed converting. On the evening of May 15, while gathering in the burned-out hollow of a majestic tree, they named themselves the Sempervirens. The group, which grew exponentially in a matter of weeks, assumed responsibility for publicizing the campaign to keep the "ever-living" but imminently threatened trees alive.

Richards, recounting the experience from his seasoned outdoorsman perspective, complimented the SCBOT for the campsite at Sinnott Creek and urged hasty action. In addition to the four mills already in operation, two more were in the process of being built, suggesting that within five years all remaining big trees would be cut. For Santa Clara County residents, what might be the consequences? Richards clearly explained the water sources on which San Jose depended: "Mountains bordering one side of Santa Clara Valley are the source of Bear Creek, San Lorenzo, Newell, and Love creeks. Northeast from this is the range in which Stevens Creek has its source." Based on previous years' experience in Boulder Creek (that is, a significant increase in logging and a major decrease in rainfall), other communities

Henry Middleton's Commercial Hotel in Boulder Creek was the starting point for the soon-to-be founders of the Sempervirens Club. The group traveled thirteen miles to their campground in Big Basin. *Courtesy of San Lorenzo Valley Museum.*

Above: W.W. Richards, secretary of the California Fish and Game Protective Association, participated in almost every Big Basin excursion, most often with his dog, King Richard. *Courtesy of Sourisseau Academy, SJSU.*

Opposite, top: Louise Jones and Carrie Walter led the way during the Santa Cruz Board of Trade's weeklong Big Basin excursion in mid-May 1900. *Courtesy History San Jose.*

Opposite, bottom: Sempervirens Club Founders (*left to right*): Louise Jones, Carrie Walter, J.Q. Packard, Charles Reed, W.W. Richards, Roley Kooser and King Richard in front row. The photographer, A.P. Hill, was also a founder. *Courtesy History San Jose.*

could expect a drastic reduction in rainfall, many times less than the annual average if the logging was not stopped.[64]

Carrie Walter and Louise Jones—having taken copious notes throughout the excursion—quickly took charge of educating the public. The *Sunday Chronicle* featured "Save the Big Basin," a full-page spread by Carrie with vivid descriptions: "In the deep canyons were trees that experts declared must be over 300 feet in height. As if in emulation of the redwoods, the firs and the madrones and other trees were giants of their kind, the product doubtless of many centuries....We found circles of giant trees standing around the space once occupied by a primeval ancestor, like children over the grave of a father....It may not be generally known, by the way, that the *Sequoia sempervirens* is the only true redwood, the (Sequoia) *gigantean* being strictly speaking not a redwood."[65]

Carrie concluded the piece in her classic poetic style: "The cry is 'Save the Trees.' Once gone, no human power or ingenuity can replace them."[66] Newspaper bylines in 1900 were almost exclusively male; but for the Big Basin campaign, journalists were women. Carrie's extensive article—concurrent with the entire SJWC joining the Sempervirens Club—led the march of activists. Louise Jones produced a rousing piece for the *San Francisco Call* in July, and Josephine McCrackin followed with "About the Big Basin" in the popular *Overland Monthly* in August.[67] Hill's photographs provided essential context for each of these articles. Meanwhile, other pieces were put in place:

July: Jeter presided over a Sempervirens Club meeting in San Jose; the group passed a resolution urging the purchase of appropriate land in Big Basin.

August: Dudley escorted Hill on a tour of the forest's core areas to help expand his knowledge and portfolio of photographs. Carrie Walter addressed a convention of school officials who adopted resolutions for a park.

September: To the Sempervirens, again gathered in San Jose, Jeter and Hill provided updates and began planning for a publicity brochure. Determined to keep the movement bipartisan, Jeter postponed future big tent meetings until after the November elections, to the dismay of some advocates.

Under the guise of a much-needed vacation, the Jeters spent the month of October traveling in and around Humboldt County, reaching out to another network: the Knights of Pythias. As the grand chancellor of the local Pythian Lodge—a fraternal organization committed to friendship, charity and benevolence—Jeter conferred with members of several lodges in the north while Jennie met with the Pythian Sisters. With a redwood-dependent economy, Humboldt residents understandably had serious concerns about the movement. The couple offered reassurance that saving Big Basin was *not* an anti-logging effort.

While touring Humboldt County in 1900, just prior to the launch of the Big Basin campaign, the Jeters experienced firsthand the alarming extent of deforestation. *Courtesy of the California State Library, Sacramento.*

They concluded their trip by traveling 150 miles by stagecoach from Eureka to Ukiah to understand the extent of redwood deforestation in the northern part of the state. Their visit to the largest lumber mill in the world—the Pacific Lumber Company—in the town of Scotia provided a firsthand look.

The mass meeting at San Francisco's Palace Hotel in November initiated preparations for the 1901 state legislative session. Dudley and Jeter's urgent request for John Muir to attend was respectfully declined. The media, the Sempervirens and other partners in the coalition heard Jeter explain the plan endorsed by the Big Basin Lumber Company (BBLC): the State of California would purchase 2,320 acres of land for $100 an acre. Moreover, the option specified that BBLC had suspended all future cutting in the immediate area.[68]

Very soon after, Dudley and other leaders agreed to escort capitalists, timber experts and educators to the proposed park. Arriving in Boulder Creek in a special parlor car, hardy souls were undeterred by "the rain coming down with a steady drip, drip, drip."[69] Middleton provided plenty

Despite heavy November rainfall, Professor Dudley (*far left*) led prominent businessmen, including bearded Duncan McPherson (*middle*), on a Big Basin exploration. *Courtesy of Santa Cruz MAH.*

of rain-proof rubber goods and several four-in-hand carriages. Over miles of muddy trails, the men finally reached their campsite deep in the forest, where they enjoyed "a feast fit for the Gods—a barbecued dinner."[70]

The storm continued the next day, but they braved the elements on horseback. Already a supporter, McPherson, the *Sentinel* editor, became a wholehearted advocate for the cause. He provided readers with details from the experience, proclaiming that Big Basin must "be saved from the ruthless woodsman" and "it cannot be duplicated on this continent."[71]

Middleton, eager to hear feedback, treated the intrepid group to a lavish farewell dinner in the warmth of his Commercial Hotel. William H. Mills, land agent for the Southern Pacific Railroad, said the land was worth only half the asking price and the state should buy all or nothing.[72] Mills didn't divulge the real agenda: if the state bought the entire area, there would be plenty of space for the railroad to build a narrow-gauge line adjacent to the park.

Moving forward with dispatch, Jeter presided over a December coalition meeting again at the Palace Hotel in San Francisco. Skilled at achieving common ground, he presented a plan for an all-out lobbying effort to pass the California Redwood Park bill. To inspire the crowd, Jeter enlisted his friend Phoebe Hearst, whose support would be a defining moment for the campaign. Their friendship had solidified while serving together on the

Right: Phoebe Apperson Hearst's "generous and timely aid and inspiration in the acquisition and development of this forest park" were the words A.A. Taylor used to describe the philanthropist's contributions. *Courtesy of History San Jose.*

Below: In May 1900, the excursionists caught 270 steelhead trout in one afternoon. The photo—used in Carrie Walter's *Woodman, Spare That Tree* brochure—helped bring sportsmen into the campaign. *Courtesy of History San Jose.*

UC Board of Regents, and they shared a special childhood bond—both grew up in working-class Missouri towns. Perhaps that contributed to their exceptional networking skills. Because Mrs. Hearst had not offered public support for the women's suffrage bill four years earlier,[73] her endorsement of the Sempervirens effort—as one of the club's vice presidents—surely made an impression. She initiated fundraising with a generous gift for creating a publicity brochure.[74]

Carrie Walter went to work writing a captivating brochure that incorporated Hill's best photographs. She titled it *Woodman Spare That Tree* from a popular song by the same name. The song's final verse conveyed the spirited determination of the movement:

> *Old Tree the storm still brave!*
> *And woodman, leave the spot;*
> *And while I have a hand to save,*
> *The axe shall have it not.*

Few people had done more to promote the natural beauty and historic structures of the region than Carrie Walter, and she insisted that saving the redwoods was one's civic duty. Not surprising, patriotic organizations such as the Native Sons and Daughters of the Golden West and pioneer societies were among the first, after the legislators, to receive the brochures, with a cover designed to look like redwood bark.

PRESERVATIONISTS
SWARM TO CAPITAL

In 1901, with automobile travel a few years away, the Sempervirens and their allies were undeterred by inconvenience. Whether by rail, steamboat or horse and buggy, they made their way to the capital, where Big Basin's future would be decided in a three-month legislative session.

The official lobbying team consisted of Hill, Jeter and Reed as the club's president, but Reed fell ill. Since Jeter, the Democrat, had a personal relationship with almost every member of the Senate, he made the necessary introductions for Hill, the Republican. Both men emphasized the bipartisan campaign, and because Jeter preferred working behind the scenes, Hill became the full-time paid lobbyist. For legislators from Southern and Central California who had scant knowledge of a redwood forest, Hill's photographs beautifully captured the essence of Big Basin.

Dudley, Walter and Hill appeared before the Committee on Public Lands and Forestry on January 4, 1901, but the media were enthralled by two other advocates. Father Robert Kenna, president of Santa Clara College, engaged lawmakers with his eloquence and humor. Mrs. E.O. Smith addressed the committee as the founder and newly elected president of the San Jose Women's Club, which was enjoying burgeoning membership. In stark contrast to her earlier lobbying role for women's suffrage, now she could emphasize the unified voice of women for the cause of preservation: "All the women…are behind this movement….The women of California love their state; they want her beauty left intact and symmetrical; the world knows us more for our big trees than for any other wonder….Don't destroy them."[75]

Mrs. E.O. Smith's tireless leadership came naturally. Like Jennie Jeter and Louise Jones, she was born into a family of abolitionists, unwavering in their commitment to equality. *Courtesy of San Jose Woman's Club, Sourisseau Academy SJSU.*

Indeed, the women involved kept their statewide networks well informed, urging them to contact legislators and keep the pressure on: Mrs. E.O. Smith with the suffragists, Carrie Walter with the Daughters of the American Revolution, Jennie Jeter with the Pythian Sisters and so on.

The momentum that seemed unstoppable hit a major snag in the Senate Finance Committee near the end of the legislative session. Senators wanted to know precisely what piece of land the state would be getting and where $250,000 would be found in an already stretched budget. With time running out, Jeter, as trustee for the Sempervirens, and Middleton, as president of the BBLC, crafted a new option that removed the major concerns.

They began by adding more acreage to the deal. Most important, the Big Basin Lumber Company, while not coming down on the asking price, agreed to receive the total payment in five $50,000 annual installments. This financial concession made it feasible for the state to purchase Big Basin, aka the California Redwood Park.

Father Kenna's ingenious approach to lobbying provided added momentum. Catholics comprised at least a quarter of the state's population, with a majority residing in the Bay Area. When Father Kenna reached out to hundreds of local priests, they in turn encouraged the faithful to contact their legislators. The well-educated Jesuit gladly said yes to Hill, his former student, who requested he make the campaign's closing argument.

On March 4, 1901, Father Kenna enthralled the standing-room-only crowd of legislators. "It is not economy but stupidity to allow the destruction of such a wonderful and unique forest, the last of its kind, which should be regarded as a priceless heritage for the people." The firm yet gentle-mannered priest perhaps reminded them of St. Francis of Assisi with his sermon on the redwoods. He went on to describe "the ravages of the lumbermen" and commented on the fact that "of this native tree, found only in this state, California did not own a single specimen."[76] He must have touched the hearts of whatever holdouts remained.

Father Kenna devoted his life to others, Catholic and non-Catholic alike. Once the park legislation passed, he celebrated at Big Basin and named this the Santa Clara Tree, known as the park's largest tree at nearly eighteen feet in diameter. *Courtesy of Special Collections SCU.*

The legislature passed the revised Redwood Park Bill of 2,500 acres at Big Basin for $100 per acre. Jeter's strategy of bipartisanship succeeded, and Father Kenna described the "wonderful enthusiasm" Hill brought to his lobbyist role as the "right man for the delicate and difficult task....Nothing disheartened him, nothing made him retreat, until the object of his heart was secured in the passage of that bill." When the funding for Hill's lobbying effort ran out, he reported having only an orange to eat and a dingy room in which to sleep but continued his commitment nonetheless.[77]

One final hurdle remained: what would it take for Governor Henry T. Gage to sign the bill? The legislature had given him an awful dilemma: two bills, each requiring large cash expenditures—Big Basin and an irrigation bill to bring much-needed water to Southern California, supported by Mills and the Southern Pacific. Depleted state coffers could barely support one initiative, even with Middleton's offer of an extended payment plan.

The Jeter-led representatives—from more than a dozen organizations and higher education institutions—besieged the governor.[78] Dudley's network of academics, many who were his fellow Sierra Club members, now showed up as an impressive mass of experts. Also well represented were the Society of California Pioneers and the Native Sons and Daughters of the Golden West. Yet despite the enormous crowd in and around his office, the governor still couldn't decide which bill to sign in late March 1901.

For the legislative campaign, Laura White had replaced Charles Reed as the Sempervirens president, and she knew how to build a winning coalition from the experience of the Calaveras campaign. Years later, she recounted what had turned the tide for Governor Gage:

> *A certain parlor of Native Daughters of the Golden West from Los Angeles had agreed to bombard the governor with telegrams, one to reach him every two minutes. He was between the devil and the deep sea. On one side, his constituency on the south, backed by the women of the south, on the other hand was a powerful corporation of water interests who eyed him with cold glances, threatening to defeat him…should he fail to do the proper thing. As the governor sat, his eyes glued on the two documents—and his soul in torture, the 150th telegram reached him from the Daughters of the South—the telegram read: "Sign the Big Basin Bill." He looked wildly around for some means of escape, some solution of the difficult problem, and then quite meekly said, "Well, I've got to sign the Big Basin [Redwood Park] bill," and forthwith affixed his name to an act which gave us what is probably the most beautiful park on the globe today.[79]*

The achievement gained attention in several parts of the country, especially from Professor Charles S. Sargent, the director of Boston's Arnold Arboretum. As a western timberlands expert, he called it a matter of national rejoicing: "The Redwood tree (*Sequoia sempervirens*) is one of the wonders of the world."[80]

THE NATIVE DAUGHTERS OF THE GOLDEN WEST PETITION TO SAVE THE BIG BASIN[*]

Transcribed by Lisa Robinson

In the Senate Monday January 28, 1901.

To the Honorable the Legislature of California:

Honorable Sirs: We, the Native Daughters of the Golden West, do most earnestly and respectfully invite your acceptance and favorable consideration of this petition relative to the preservation of the forests of California.

As native daughters, both as an order, through our grand officers, and as individuals (as witness the signatures to our petition), we indorse the work of the Sempervirens Club, and implore your aid to secure the preservation, in the form of a Government park, of the wonderful primeval forest of coast redwood known as the "Big Basin," and its immediate environments, located in the Santa Cruz Mountains; a solid body of magnificent redwood—the oldest specimens of plant life known.

We call upon you, our worthy and trusted representatives, to give your effective aid to this patriotic project, either by appropriating sufficient money from the State Treasury to purchase the land outright, or by instituting condemnation proceedings on the ground of public utility; in brief, to set in motion the machinery of the law immediately to save these forests from destruction.

The welfare of our entire State depends upon the prosperity of each and every section. The "Big Basin" lies in the counties of Santa Cruz and San Mateo. Its destruction means the lessening of the rainfall of Central California, and the loss of the water supply
(continued on next page)

---

[*] *The Journal of the Senate During the Thirty-Fourth Session of the Legislature of the State of California*, 1901 (Sacramento: A.J. Johnson, Superintendent State Printing, 1901), 272.

of Santa Cruz, San Mateo, and Santa Clara Counties, and of the City of San Francisco. This would be a public calamity. We pray you to avert it by saving to us, to our beloved California, and to the generations yet to come, this magnificent forest—the growth of many centuries.

For the honor of California, we are

Yours respectfully,

Ema Gett, Grand President; Genevieve Baker, Grand Vice-President; Laura J. Frakes, Grand Secretary; Dora Zmudowski, Grand Treasurer; Harriett Stoddard Lee, Grand Trustee; Mamie A. Ryan, Grand Trustee; Emma G. Foley, Grand Trustee; Stella A.H. Finkeldey, Grand Trustee; Mary J. Langford, Grand Trustee; and 1,000 members of the order.

In the years that followed the victory, William Jeter and Louise Jones consistently called it a remarkable team effort. But that characterization had no staying power. Some years later, historian Edward L. Martin published a piece on the competition for laurels titled "Who Saved the Big Basin?":

> "I" said Duncan McPherson, "for I went there in person."
> "Not much," said J.F. Coope. "It was my gentle whoop that saved the Big Basin."
> "I'm not giving you a fill," said A.P. Hill. "What else could be truer with my camera obscura? I saved the Big Basin."
> "Nay," said Professor Dudley, fresh from the campus,
> "I was once pinched for a trampus. With my dissertation, I saved the Big Basin."
> "Listen to me," said George Radcliff. "Me and Senator Tom Flint
> gave the governor a hint that saved the Big Basin."
> "Come off," said Governor Gage,
> "twas my pen on the page that saved the Big Basin."

According to Martin, "Every one that ever heard of the Big Basin seemed to come forward and insist that *he* was the savior of this forest park."[81]

Laura Lovell White, second president of the Sempervirens Club, wrote several articles for *Overland Monthly* and received accolades for protecting the Calaveras Big Trees. *Courtesy of Mill Valley Public Library, Lucretia Little History Room.*

Laura White endeavored to set the record straight to an international audience in 1915. She presented a paper for Sempervirens Day at the San Francisco Pan-American Pacific Exposition to make the point: "We together, men and women, worked hand-in-hand for the accomplishment of the same supreme object—the acquisition of the State Redwood Park."[82]

Phoebe Hearst had won a place in the leadership structure for the Exposition—thanks in part to Laura White's support—and William Hearst's *Examiner* reported his mother's considerable victory for women. For White—who had begun her public speaking decades earlier as a suffragist—the 1915 Exposition would be her final talk. After taking a strong stand for the indispensable role of women in saving Big Basin, she passed on a few months later.

UNFORESEEN OBSTACLES

Why did it take three years and three months after the passage of the California Redwood Park bill for Big Basin to officially open? The bipartisan unity, essential to the legislative success, collapsed, and newspapers battled one another over specifics of the land purchase.

S oon after signing the legislation, Governor Gage selected four men to serve with him on the Big Basin Park Commission, with representation from Santa Cruz County conspicuously absent. Sempervirens applauded the appointments of Professor Dudley and Father Kenna, revered academic leaders. The other two appointees represented railroad interests: A.W. Foster, president and owner of the Northwestern Pacific line, and William H. (aka W.H.) Mills of the Southern Pacific. Railroads had opposed whatever public land decisions would negatively impact their timber holdings and/or plans for expansion. In addition, the Southern Pacific enjoyed an outsized influence in the Republican Party, which Gage hoped would nominate him for a second term.

The five commissioners faced a momentous decision: which 2,500 acres of more than 14,000 from which to choose should the state purchase with the appropriated funds? Meeting for the first time in June, they decided to inspect Big Basin for themselves. Along with regional experts, they scheduled a five-day camping visit for early August 1901. The *Sentinel* predicted they would quickly finalize a deal.

The Sempervirens Club wanted to be on hand to introduce Governor Gage to the park, but fearing fire, Middleton had placed the land off-

For their 1901 celebratory camping trip, the Sempervirens hired Jacob Overton to cater the event. Overton, with his close friend Reverend George Jackson of the African Methodist Episcopal Zion Church in San Jose, is at the far right. *Courtesy of Santa Cruz MAH.*

limits. Hill appealed the decision and won permission for an encampment to coincide with the arrival of the commissioners. The preservationists' small caravan rolled from Boulder Creek to Big Basin on August 5, with Hill driving the lead carriage and Carrie Walter as a passenger. The rest of the party, which didn't include Jeter or Dudley, rode in wagons carrying baggage, tents, cooking equipment and ten days' supply of food. They disembarked at a place known as Slippery Rock and established Sempervirens Camp.[83]

On their second day, the previous day's *San Francisco Call* arrived from town, shocking Carrie and her fellow campers. An exposé therein insinuated the much-too-expensive park project would enable the timber owners, particularly Timothy Hopkins, to loot the public purse.[84]

Based on an anonymous source inside the commission, the *Call*'s story questioned the club's judgment for championing an appropriation that far exceeded the true value of the trees. The inaccessibility of the Big Basin tract alone, the article suggested, should have disqualified it. The campers were indignant, and their reporter friends at the *San Jose Mercury* believed hostile influencers were at work.

The next shoe dropped later in the week, when the commissioners voted to postpone their visit. One of their members, evidently Mills, told the *Call* that the tracts belonging to Timothy Hopkins were overpriced, and furthermore, they would not deal with the Sempervirens Club. Some other

Jacob Overton prepared the Sempervirens' meals from his "kitchen," an oversized tent. Louise Jones sits at the front right with Overton at the back right. *Courtesy of History San Jose.*

Bay Area papers joined the criticism, while Santa Cruz editors staunchly defended the Big Basin Lumber Company.

Despite their deflated enthusiasm, the Sempervirens enjoyed one noteworthy bright spot during their camping trip. Reverend George Jackson of the African Methodist Episcopal Zion Church in San Jose had come to Big Basin to help his friend Jacob Overton, a well-known chef and events caterer. When some in the club learned their chef's helper was a minister, they invited him to give the park's first public sermon. All of the campers gathered around the roaring fire to hear the impromptu address. Reverend Jackson's Bible reference—"Unto us a child is born and his name shall be called wonderful"—was appropriate for the diversity of denominations. He then spoke of the trees and concluded by sharing his hope for the future: "Through religion and education should come real freedom for the Black man."

While some commissioners dawdled, Father Kenna made a solo trip to the proposed park, taking pains to examine the heart of the area. His conclusion

Right: The Reverend George Jackson, minister of the First African Methodist Episcopal Zion Church in San Jose, attributed the good education he received to support from Reverend Henry Ward Beecher of New York. *Courtesy of San Jose Mercury News, June 8, 1903.*

Below: To inspect Big Basin, Governor Henry Gage (*center*) is joined by Commissioners Kenna (*next to Gage on left*), Dudley (*fourth from Gage on left*) and W.H. Mills (*on Dudley's right*) as well as various experts. Duncan McPherson is second from the end on right. *Courtesy of Santa Cruz MAH.*

echoed the sentiment of Harvard botanist Charles Sargent, who called it the noblest of forests. Father Kenna told the Boulder Creek paper, "It is grand beyond description…far exceeded what I expected and it will be a shame if it's not saved from destruction."[85] The commission as a whole arrived in mid-September at the Governor's Camp, made possible by the generosity of Hopkins and Middleton, who endeavored to keep the area as pristine as possible. The site, accessible only by horse or mule, consisted of a large cabin with bedrooms and a dining hall with an attached kitchen.

The commissioners and their experts explored the basin in detail, and after dinner, indulging in wine and cigars, they studied Dudley's maps. While they expressed much satisfaction, it didn't translate into action. At the commission's next meeting in early October, W.H. Mills again claimed $100 per acre was a great deal too much to pay and believed one or two other commissioners agreed.

With the commission at a standstill, women stepped in and showcased the immense value of the park. With Middleton's blessing, Jennie Jeter orchestrated a two-week, multi-family camping trip to celebrate the recreational splendor of the soon-to-be-open park. But knowing a full day's travel from Santa Cruz would be too strenuous for the children, she invited the entire group to spend their first night at her brother Frank Bliss's summer home in Brookdale, fifteen miles from the destination. A bucolic area where timber cutting had permanently stopped five years earlier, it would soon be called the gateway to Big Basin and become a Mecca for second homes. (In the years to come, tourists and celebrities thronged to the idyllic Brookdale Lodge.)

The families comprising Jennie's camping trip—Hopkins, Deming, and Reverend Pon Fang—conveyed a joyful message: California Redwood Park belongs to everyone, especially parents and their children. Pon Fang was well known as both a Santa Cruz merchant and a teacher of English for Chinese residents. His friendship with Jennie and the Demings had blossomed through their shared commitment to the Congregational Church's Chinese Mission where he served as a leader. It's hard to imagine that Reverend Pon Fang didn't give a sermon or two during the group's time in Big Basin.

That same month, Louise Jones produced an extensive account of the Sempervirens' August campout for the *San Jose Herald*, with a reprint in the *Evening Sentinel*.[86] Offering vivid details about the trails, trees and stunning array of flowers, her article beckoned readers to explore the transcendent landscapes of Big Basin. She believed that day was not far off.

Victorian-era writers who attempted to capture the redwoods' ineffable quality often sounded grandiloquent. Yet Jones's words, from years of experience as a journalist, often writing about nature, resonated: "In this vast laboratory nature distills a balm for hurts, a subtle essence that heals and soothes; as we breathe the freshness and fragments of the air we receive also strength and hope from some divine and hidden source. The things of time and sense lose their power over us....The fetters of custom and conventionality fall away: we taste soul freedom and feel intimations of immortality."[87]

Jennie Jeter's (*far left*) camping trip for Santa Cruz families featured William Jeter and Reverend Pon Fang (*far right*) serving as the chefs. Pon Fang's son (*middle, front*) and the other children were among the very first known to camp at Big Basin. *Courtesy of Santa Cruz MAH.*

By November 1901, with no word yet from the commission, owners Hopkins and Middleton very quietly spent the night in Big Basin. But for what purpose? Did they discuss the revised offer Middleton had signaled to the commission: to add another seven hundred acres of cutover land? Or did Hopkins have something even bigger in mind?

The commission had still failed to act by the beginning of 1902. Carrie Walter, knowing that the battle would be won or lost in the media, provided an eight-hundred-word piece to the *Sacramento Bee.* Writing as the Sempervirens secretary, she began with the headline "Letter from the people: A Plea for the Big Basin Redwood Park." She pulled no punches, providing a detailed account of the club's efforts to arrive at a fair estimate of the trees' value and to secure the original purchase option, which had recently expired. While appealing to public spirit, patriotism and Mr. Mills's best self, Walter would not stand for the *Call* labeling Sempervirens sentimental enthusiasts: "Fault finders of our work stayed away from the Big Basin and threw cold water upon our efforts. The club has worked unfaltering to give to California the most wonderful, the most unique forest park on earth, one that will make our state the Mecca of tourists, scientists and wonder seekers for all time. We naturally do not enjoy being accused of selfish or mercenary or even foolish impulses under the circumstances."[88]

Back when the movement officially began at Stanford in 1900, Jeter made Dudley's expertise center stage. Now two and a half years later, the duo operated in concert once again at a Sempervirens Park Convention. To a packed house at First Unitarian Church in San Jose, Dudley made clear that his remarks were not given as a commissioner. Instead, with his comprehensive firsthand knowledge, the botanist asked the assembly to be patient and allow the commission to achieve a satisfactory conclusion.[89]

The anxious crowd then heard from the acclaimed orator and San Jose defense lawyer Delphin Delmas. Though it would be another five years before he would achieve international fame as the defense attorney in a notorious murder trial in New York, his persuasive skills were already legendary. He forcefully countered the newspaper accounts that called the owners of Big Basin Lumber Company mercenaries. Applauding their generosity, he

Mrs. E.O. Smith, a benefactor of the First Unitarian Church at 160 North Third Street in San Jose, made possible its use by the San Jose Woman's Club, including for Big Basin advocacy. *Courtesy Sourriseau Academy SJSU.*

In early 1901, Henry Middleton (*front left*) gave San Jose attorney D.M. Delmas (*front right*) a tour of Big Basin. Shown here near Slippery Rock, the excursion prepared Delmas for his upcoming address to the legislature. *Courtesy of History San Jose.*

noted they had stuck with the original deal when "the value of the land had increased double, triple and quadruple."[90] Delmas, with his firsthand knowledge of the park, brought the crowd to a fever pitch. Jeter, by contrast, hoped to calm them down by reinforcing Dudley's position and endorsing the commission's work. If anyone in the media suspected the two of working on some new plan behind closed doors, it didn't get reported.

Continued media skepticism over the asking price, no doubt fueled by the Southern Pacific, created an unlikely alliance. In Santa Cruz, longtime rivals Taylor, the Democrat, and McPherson, the Republican, had exchanged hostilities via their newspapers' editorials. When they sniped at each other over the park, Taylor accused the *Sentinel* owner of being way late to the game, and McPherson seemed dismissive of the photography and reporting Frederick Clarke had done early on for Taylor's *Surf*. Now, however, the two newspapermen united in defense of the Big Basin owners as fair-minded men with honest motives.

A.A. Taylor arrived in Santa Cruz in the late 1870s and consolidated local papers to create the *Surf*. His decades of commitment to preserving Big Basin began in the late 1880s. Courtesy *of Santa Cruz MAH*.

But an alliance of small-town papers was no match for the big city *Call* and its unabashed criticism of the proposed deal.[91] The media ruckus enabled Mills, now chair of the commission, to continue the delay. Finally, he made his big play by requesting the attorney general's opinion on the body's powers and limitations. In early June, the AG responded by confirming the intent of the legislature: the commission was authorized to pay the full amount requested at a rate of $50,000 a year over five years.

By this time, McPherson had attended more park-related events than any other editor in the state; he wanted the details firsthand and made sure he got them. Now he eagerly reprinted the *Call*'s lead story: "Big Basin Park now a certainty, commissioners decide to buy the Santa Cruz County property."[92] But the good report proved premature. Neither Father Kenna nor Dudley could risk a vote by the commission without a guarantee of it passing. Unity had been the movement's hallmark. They needed a game changer. It came when Father Kenna personally invoked one of the most powerful newspapers in the state.

How a Jesuit Priest Turns the Tide

During the first half of the twentieth century, a few newspaper-owning families virtually ran the Golden State.[93] The Sacramento Bee *was the state's progressive voice, and by 1883, the anti-monopoly McClatchy family owned the paper with Charles McClatchy (twenty-four) serving as editor. In the years to come, Charles would be an outstanding voice for conservation and the appropriate use of public land as well as other progressive causes.[94]*

Father Kenna now turned to his good friend Charles McClatchy, who had sided with some other Bay Area editors against the Big Basin purchase price. The priest later provided a firsthand account of what transpired that July 1902.

McClatchy agreed to "change the tone of the Bee if I could prove to him that the price asked was not excessive. I accepted his terms and we both went into the heart of the Big Basin and on showing him figures and documents and bringing experienced experts to prove that the land was worth more by at least $100,000 than the price demanded...he came out with the noble apology....Prepared to withstand the threatened attack of the bay press, his noble action completely silenced them."

The seasoned editor described his Saul-like conversion with awe: "The land set aside for park purposes presents as magnificent a stretch of beautiful and sublime landscape as the sun ever shown upon."[95]

Back in the land of preservationists, many were chomping at the bit to experience the people's park. Hill organized an August camping experience for more than fifty guests at the Sempervirens Camp. A month later, in early September, a Chinese cook greeted the San Francisco–based Sierra Club at the Governor's Camp. For a decade, Dudley had kept the group informed about Big Basin; now twenty members collectively spoke out with a formal resolution for the commission and the media:

Charles K. McClatchy, the owner/editor of the *Sacramento Bee*, had a "Saul-like" conversion experience once he experienced Big Basin for himself, thanks to Father Kenna. *Courtesy of Santa Cruz Public Library.*

> *Resolved, that after three days of wide inspection of the Big Basin, we recognize the great good that will come to the people of the State by its purchase of the property as proposed, which we find contains a grandly beautiful forest of great redwoods and other valuable trees.*[96]

Two weeks later, on September 20, the commissioners convened at the Palace Hotel for the momentous occasion. On behalf of the citizens of California, they made the purchase for $250,000, despite Mills's strong objection and what Hearst called his "bad grace" in the *Examiner*. What took the media by complete surprise was the final amount of acreage—an additional 1,300 acres of cut-over land contributed by Hopkins and Middleton, owners of the Big Basin Lumber Company. Experts called the amount of marketable lumber in the total acreage remarkable: 135 million feet.

Hearst wrote a lengthy and exuberant piece: "It will become not only one of the greatest attractions in the vicinity of San Francisco but a much talked of public resort the world over."[97] Father Kenna said, "It was a glorious victory for the Sempervirens Club.…But to Stanford University and Santa Clara College are due special credit for the success since they were always in the heat of the battle on the fighting line."[98]

The Sierra Club—on their 1902 Big Basin camping trip—took action to support the park's purchase price. W.W. Richards led the group as Professor Dudley (*third from front*) mingled with fellow members and their spouses. *Courtesy of Santa Cruz MAH.*

But the rival *Chronicle* denigrated the expansion to 3,800 acres because of its higher cost to maintain. "Sentimentalists care nothing for expense and schemers know how to work sentimentalists by encouraging their sentimentalism."[99]

Charles McClatchy gave special accolades to Father Kenna. As soon as news of the purchase broke, the *Sacramento Bee* posted his picture on the

From 1900 to 1904, most Big Basin–related meetings were held at San Francisco's Palace Hotel, built in 1875 with Leland Stanford as the first to sign the register. The 1906 earthquake and aftermath destroyed the iconic structure. *Courtesy of San Francisco Public Library.*

front page with the caption "The man who got the Big Basin for the state of California." The article described "his untiring and persistent work… as always in the interest of the people. He continued the battle before the legislature when others had given up in despair and it was proper that his motion on Wednesday last in the meeting of the commissioners should consummate the work in which he had been unselfishly engaged for several years."[100] Though Father Kenna had to resign from the commission due to ill health, he continued advocating for the park. He wanted easy access for all, especially the poor.

It had been seventeen months from the time the California Redwood Park bill was signed into law until the official purchase was agreed upon in September 1902. How soon would the public get access?

A Governor Who Believes in the Cause

Governor George Pardee gave his wholehearted support to Warden Humphrey Pilkington during the 1904 fire. Afterward, the governor fought unsuccessfully for a statewide fire prevention master plan. *Courtesy of Society of California Pioneers, San Francisco.*

José DeLaveaga's commitment to a natural landscape on his bucolic estate provided extensive experience for landscaper Humphrey Pilkington, Big Basin's heroic first warden. *Courtesy of Sutter's Fort State Historic Park, Sacramento.*

By this time, many of California's Republicans had become embarrassed by Gage's performance as governor. Dr. George Pardee became the compromise candidate between reform-minded Republicans aligned with President Roosevelt and the "railroad" Republicans. Pardee, the first governor to be born in California, brought his passion for conserving natural resources to the job. Moreover, as a former mayor of Oakland, he had refused to back down when challenged by the Southern Pacific.

For Father Kenna's replacement on the commission, Pardee selected a man who, like his predecessor, could be counted on to serve the forest's best interests. H.F. Kron was his classmate from UC Berkeley and a highly respected Santa Cruz businessman. Kron, like Timothy Hopkins, represented a new generation of civic-minded sons in twentieth-century California. His father, founder of the San Lorenzo Tannery in the 1860s, had decimated tan oak forests harvesting the trees' bark for his leather-tanning process. It produced a heartbreaking sight. "Although labor was saved by not felling the tree, the peeled tan oak eventually died standing."[101]

For the first park warden, Pardee selected another friend from his UC Berkeley days, J.H.B. Pilkington. A fruit farm owner in Santa Cruz with considerable expertise in horticulture, Humphrey, as he was known, studied trees in college and used organic methods of soil enrichment. His abilities had been well established locally as the director of design, planting and maintenance on the vast estate of his neighbor, José Vincente DeLaveaga. The nearly six hundred acres—with groves of fruit and nut trees and several meandering streams—reflected DeLaveaga's love of nature.

Initially, Big Basin had this one official park building. Located at Governor's Camp, it consisted of five individual sleeping rooms equipped with standard beds and bedding. *Courtesy of the Santa Cruz MAH.*

When he died in 1894, he left the bucolic estate to the city and county of Santa Cruz, which named it DeLaveaga Park.[102]

In July 1903, Pilkington began his term as warden with a monthly salary of $125. Imagine Middleton's delight to have turned over all park maintenance to Pilkington, who on July 25, welcomed the Pardee and Kron families for an extended stay. The governor and the commissioner had camped in the area many years earlier as college students. Now the two officeholders walked together the few miles from Sempervirens Camp to the Governor's Camp. With the details of the land transfer at last complete, the people of California had full ownership of the Big Basin redwood forest and a warden they could count on.

7

OPENED AT LAST BUT CATASTROPHE LOOMS

W arden Pilkington carefully walked the park's entire circumference in spring 1904, prompted by fire concerns from the previous year. At the behest of the commissioners, he ordered more dry brush cleared and additional trails constructed before the June grand opening of California Redwood Park—the official name. As hoped for, the opening brought hordes of exuberant tourists, arriving in their four-in-hand buggies. Their commemorative postcards went far and wide, boasting of a pristine forest replete with creeks, breathtaking waterfalls and all manner of wildlife. Splendid accounts undoubtedly provided a beacon of hope for forest preservation nationwide.

At the end of the season, many Sempervirens again gathered at the Unitarian Church in San Jose. Together with the San Jose Women's Club, they bid farewell to one of their most influential members, Mrs. E.O. Smith. Louise Jones gave a moving eulogy, and Carrie Walter read her poem "In Memory of Mrs. E.O. Smith."[103] The media's obituary, though lauding a life committed to civic causes, made no mention of Mrs. Smith's activism on behalf of the park. As it happened, that same week marked the beginning of an unimaginable stretch of bad luck for the trees.

Following several days of record heat—one hundred degrees throughout Santa Cruz County—a terrifying fire originated at the Waterman Mill on Pescadero Creek in San Mateo County. It raged toward the park's interior,

The original entrance gate to Big Basin stated the goal of the preservationists: "To Be Preserved in a State of Nature." That language lasted at least until the 1920s. *Courtesy Frank Perry Collection.*

Duncan McPherson, Carrie Walter and Fredrick W. Billing (*driving*) were among those arriving at the park in style when it finally opened in June 1904. Their location is not far from where the Old Lodge would be built in 1915. *Courtesy of Santa Cruz MAH.*

Boulder Creek Stage, Redwood Park, Santa Cruz

Above: July 4, 1908. Though automobiles had a convenient paved road from Boulder Creek to Big Basin by 1906, visitors often sought the thrill of a stagecoach ride into the park. *Courtesy of Ross Eric Gibson Collection.*

Right: Carrie Stevens Walter, the most prolific writer for the movement, stood up to naysayers. Although her family donated this A.P. Hill portrait to Big Basin, it was never displayed and was eventually stored in Sacramento. Consequently, it survived the 2020 inferno. (See page 153.) *Courtesy Statewide Museum Collections Center, California State Parks, Sacramento.*

Above: Newspaper owner/editor Duncan McPherson commissioned A.P. Hill to create this oil painting for San Francisco's Pan Pacific Exhibition in 1915. Three women, members of the McPherson family, admire the 1,800-year-old Father Tree. *Courtesy of Robert Bettencourt, History San Jose.*

Right: Up until the late 1970s, folks of all ages delighted to feed the Big Basin deer with bags of oats from a concessionaire. Contestants at the Miss California Pageant, held annually in Santa Cruz, always received a tour of Big Basin and a warm welcome from the wildlife, as shown here. *Author's Collection.*

The burgeoning popularity of deer feeding evolved into a buck's head appearing on every type of park souvenir from spoon holders to teacups. China plates, displaying multiple views of the park, were among the most sought-after mementoes. *Courtesy of Ronnie Trubeck Collection.*

For several decades, the Calling of the Deer occurred daily at 4:30 p.m. Performing this cherished feeding ritual, the assistant warden called "come babe" through his megaphone. Thrilled tourists watched as deer made their way down from the mountains. *Courtesy of Frank Perry Collection.*

The Civilian Conservation Corps' expansion of the Campfire Center ("Bowl") in 1935 included this fancy stage. Subsequently, the Big Basin Lodge advertised "Evening campfire programs featuring educational talks and local talent give delight to nearly one thousand persons nightly." *Courtesy of Ross Eric Gibson Collection.*

The Sempervirens Fund made a major contribution to upgrading the Campfire Center in 2009, installing all new redwood benches providing for ADA access and greater comfort. The structure accommodated a variety of uses in a naturalistic setting. *Courtesy of Bill Rhoades Collection.*

Left: Acclaimed landscape artist and teacher Santa Cruz native Frank Heath produced this stunning oil painting during the early 1900s. Other Heath originals of Big Basin burned in the Zayante Inn fire of 1921. *Courtesy of United Methodist Church of Santa Cruz Collection.*

Below: This etching, by artist W.A. Lambrecht, hung in Jennie Bliss Jeter's dining room at Cliff Crest. She named it *The Path*—her daily reminder of the importance of making the Santa Cruz Mountain redwoods accessible to everyone. *Author's Collection.*

Above: The North Highway 236 entrance passes a sweeping view of the park. In the distance are Pine Mountain and Mount McAbee. Below them: park headquarters, campgrounds and trails. Originally known as the Saratoga-Big Basin Road, it opened in time for San Francisco's 1915 Panama-Pacific Exposition. *Courtesy of Bill Rhoades Collection.*

Left: The beautiful Five Finger Fern is one of many species found adjacent to the streams and waterfalls. Indigenous people's practical use of the park's ferns ranged from their highly skilled basket weaving to roofing to the linings of their earth ovens and acorn leaching pits. *Courtesy of Bill Rhoades Collection.*

Above: The Civilian Conservation Corps built the park headquarters in 1936. The historic building also served as the park's visitor center, located a short distance from the park store, museum and many trails, including the popular Redwood Loop. *Courtesy of Bill Rhoades Collection.*

Right: Visitors admire the Mother Tree's dramatic height, which for decades was measured at 329 feet. They are also intrigued by the large hollow opening. Called goose pens (aka fire caves), these natural features were used by the earliest visitors to store their outdoor equipment during the park's winter closures. *Courtesy of Bill Rhoades Collection.*

This fallen ancient giant rests on the Redwood Loop Trail along Opal Creek. A wonder of nature is the redwood's wide root system that becomes interlaced with neighboring trees. That underground structure helps trees of such height survive storms and intense winds. *Courtesy of Bill Rhoades Collection.*

Annually, costumed volunteers perform their Founders Day Celebration standing at stations along the Redwood Loop. As the "melodrama" moves through the forest, visitors listen to voices from yesteryear. Estrella and Jerry Bibbey, Big Basin docents for twenty years, sit at the Mother Tree. *Courtesy of Bill Rhoades Collection.*

Above: The historic Redwood Loop Trail is ADA compliant, comfortably providing wheelchair and stroller access. The 0.6-mile self-guided tour of breathtaking old-growth redwood trees includes some of the largest trees in the park. *Courtesy of Bill Rhoades Collection*.

Left: Berry Creek Falls, named for a lumberman who built his cabin near the base 140 years ago, is a treasure deep in the Santa Cruz Mountains. Silver and Golden Falls are part of the trio that enchants visitors along the eleven-mile Berry Creek Falls Loop. *Courtesy of Bill Rhoades Collection.*

Above: Passing a freshwater marshland entering Rancho del Oso, just ahead on the left is the new welcome center. It features innovative nature and orientation exhibits thanks to a grant from Save the Redwoods League and the Waddell Creek Association. *Courtesy of Bill Rhoades Collection.*

Left: At the stunning Golden Falls, seasonal iron oxide coloring appears as nature's artwork. Below it is the Cascades, another vibrant slope showcasing how each waterfall on the Berry Creek trail is distinctive. *Courtesy of Bill Rhoades Collection.*

In 2011, not far from park headquarters, Tim Hyland, environmental scientist for California State Parks, elaborated on the ecology of old-growth redwood forests with district staff members. Docent/historian Traci Bliss (*with binoculars*) participated as an invited guest. (See epilogue, page 148.) *Courtesy of Bill Rhoades Collection.*

Spring through summer, the western azalea is probably the most enjoyed aroma in the forest. *Rhododendron occidentale* "rose-tree of the Western sky" aptly describes the unusually tall shrub, native only to the region west of the Sierra. Nestled here against the Washington tree, roots will resprout after severe nature events. *Courtesy of Bill Rhoades Collection.*

Left: A young family enjoys Blooms Creek Campground, aptly named for the nearby creek that was once the site of the Historic Bloom's Mill. Only a half-mile from the park headquarters, in summertime this area is surrounded by delicious native huckleberries. *Courtesy of Bill Rhoades Collection.*

Below: The lightning strikes of 2:29 a.m. on August 16, 2020, ignited the CZU Lightning Complex fire that would consume Big Basin three days later. This view is of West Cliff Drive leading to Steamers Lane in Santa Cruz. *Courtesy of Shmuel Thaler Collection.*

"Driving toward Big Basin at 9 p.m., August 18, I knew the bright orange glow above Highway 236 meant devastation and trauma. I'd photographed many wildfires as a *Sentinel* photographer, but nothing prepared me for the fierceness and unpredictability of this one." *Courtesy of Shmuel Thaler Collection.*

Professional tree feller Bruce Baker of Brookdale felt like he had lost a close friend seeing this charred Big Basin entrance sign on August 24, 2020. For decades, visitors had requested his help taking pictures at this junction: Upper Highway 236 and China Grade. *Courtesy of Bruce Baker.*

This page: The Big Basin Museum before and after the 2020 fire. The new Nature Museum and Research Center, years in the making, would have opened to the public in spring 2021. In the foreground is the building's chimney, which cracked during the 1989 Loma Prieta earthquake. *Courtesy of Friends of Santa Cruz State Parks. (See page 149.)*

Above: A veteran firefighter and photographer, SLV Steve captured this scene on October 3 on China Grade—a half mile from the park. "For the whole first two months, we encountered flaming trees like this every single day." *Courtesy of SLV Steve Collection.*

Left: Archaeologist Mark Hylkema—supervisor Cultural Resources Program and Tribal Liaison, California State Parks—surveys the historical remains of Big Basin's old lodge, built in 1915. Early visitors to the park arrived by horse and carriage for fine dining in what had been the oldest remaining park building. *Courtesy of Mark Hylkema Collection.*

Left: Seen here visiting the historic Slippery Rock area, the usually shy pileated woodpecker is the show stealer of the old growth forest. These birds fill the forest with an unmistakable sound as they hammer away to create large rectangular openings high in the tree trunks. *Courtesy of Bill Rhoades Collection.*

Below: In May 2021, the westernmost edge of Big Basin reopened to the public, where the twenty-nine-mile Skyline to the Sea trail starts. Rancho Del Oso interpreter Richard Fletcher explains to visitors the marshland's rich biodiversity with Monterey Bay National Marine Sanctuary in the background. *Courtesy of Bill Rhoades Collection.*

Caroline Pilkington (*foreground*) and her friends evacuated the Governor's Camp during the 1904 fire. They dropped their pets at Bloom's Mill before continuing the arduous walk to safety in Boulder Creek. *Courtesy of San Lorenzo Valley Museum.*

home to the largest old growth trees and the two campgrounds. When the report reached Pilkington at two o'clock in the morning on September 8, he immediately headed out, leaving his wife, Caroline, her two cousins and three friends from San Jose. The women stayed put at the Governor's Camp, reassuring themselves that surely the fire wouldn't reach them.

Just before noon, weeks of fresh mountain air and tranquility abruptly ended. Lumbermen from Bloom's Mill insisted on a hasty evacuation, giving the women just enough time to secure their trunks between boulders in the creek bed and cover them with wet blankets. Then, braving the blinding dust and smoke, the campers walked at least a dozen miles over rugged mountain terrain to Boulder Creek.[104]

Once in town, the women learned that several fires burned throughout the entire county in addition to those in the Santa Cruz Mountains. They'd

I.T. Bloom, seen here with a log fourteen feet in diameter, helped save Big Basin from the 1904 fire. He quickly dispatched his lumbermen to act as firefighters. *Courtesy of Special Collections UCSC.*

seen firsthand the conflagration "cutting a wide-burned channel through the heart of the park." What must have run through Caroline Pilkington's mind when she heard the other report? Though reinforcements had reached her husband, he needed many dozens more to save the park. When Governor Pardee told him "spare no cost," Pilkington offered a very generous hourly wage to anyone who signed up. Few did. Who would willingly enter a "veritable furnace" with no means of communication?

The warden, himself unreachable, continued to dispatch pleas for help. In less than forty-eight hours, private sector interests jumped to his aid. The Bloom's Mill lumbermen and the Southern Pacific's track crews, men who knew the terrain, comprised the surge of additional firefighters. The warden, going several days without sleep or a change of clothes, directed the brigade at the park's northeastern edge.

STANFORD COMES THROUGH

But who was tending to the western slope where the fire began? Professor and Park Commissioner Dudley—the one person who knew specific details of Big Basin topography—organized a twelve-member squad of Stanford University athletes. Mostly upperclassmen from the Delta Upsilon fraternity, the team also included his nephew Ernest and President Jordan's son Harold. The volunteers, strong and fit, had one indispensable qualification in common: each had participated in Dudley's survey of the park's landscape.

Harold Jordan, son of Stanford's president, was one of a dozen student volunteers whose efforts stopped the 1904 fire from burning the Pescadero Woods. *Courtesy of Special Collections Stanford.*

The Stanford Relief Expedition, as they were called, left campus at 4:30 p.m. a few hours before Caroline Pilkington and her companions reached Boulder Creek. Embracing their extraordinary mission, the students delivered essential supplies to engulfed firefighters and built a fire wall at Pescadero Creek. Ten days later, Dudley expressed his gratitude at a press briefing: "It was solely through the efforts of the party that the fire was prevented from crossing the Pescadero ridge on Saturday, in which case the famous Pescadero woods would have been destroyed." Dudley also reported that the ancient redwoods in the heart of Big Basin were intact.[105]

He lauded Pilkington's leadership and bravery in containing the fire, which was mostly under control by September 15. When the commissioners convened, they made clearing underbrush a number one priority, though that task was already at the top of the warden's list.

Estimates of how many fires had burned simultaneously in the Santa Cruz Mountains ranged from six to twenty, but none had converged—a major factor in saving the forest. Hundreds of acres of chaparral were gone, and the fire seared a strip of fine redwood timber on the eastern edge. Fortunately, with a downpour on September 27, the media announced all of the fires were contained.[106]

But the relatively short fire produced big consequences. In early 1905, the legislature sought to abolish the Park Commission and place Big Basin under a state board of forestry consisting of the secretary of state, the attorney general and the secretary of the State Board of Examiners, with the governor serving as chairman.

Pardee championed the bill because of a key provision: a comprehensive approach to fire management he believed essential to California's future. The state forester, appointed by the board, would have authority to compel all owners of forest land to adopt measures for their preservation and for the extinguishing of forest fires. But Pardee's long-standing adversary, the Southern Pacific, made certain no one would regulate its vast land holdings. "The bill was shorn of its most effective provisions before being allowed to pass," Pardee lamented.[107] In fact the gutting of the bill wreaked untold havoc as Taylor later described: "Thus it came to pass that politics like the serpent of old entered the garden of the gods bringing indifference, neglect and graft in its trail."[108]

Meanwhile, Warden Pilkington replaced the two burned out bridges at the park so that tourism could resume. On July 15, 1905, just ten months after the fire, an eager public poured in once again. The Governor's Camp, with its deeply shaded area on the south fork of Waddell Creek, quickly filled

The summer after the fire, Florence Hill (*left*) and friends celebrated the park's reopening. That year, 1905, the American flag had forty-five stars. *Courtesy of History San Jose.*

to capacity, as did the Sempervirens Camp, once the favorite spot of deer hunters. According to Taylor, the 2,500 people who came to the park that year saw a verdurous landscape owing to an abundant rainfall: "Vegetation sprang from the earth with more than Phoenix-like vitality."[109]

Though the park successfully reopened, access remained barely suitable for wagons. Santa Cruz County supervisors stepped up with a commitment to modernity—a new road to replace the rough, potholed one from Boulder Creek. The cement thoroughfare would provide efficient access for future firefighters and usher in the advent of automobiles. Imagine a tourist's thrill gazing up at the redwood canopy from an open-air touring car.

THE GREAT URBAN DISASTER

In 1906, Pilkington's ongoing fire recovery efforts, wholeheartedly supported by Governor Pardee, provided realistic hope for a robust summer season. The opening of the car-worthy road would bring scores of day visitors for the first time and reinvigorate the San Lorenzo Valley economy. Instead, attendance plummeted: an out-of-control urban fire threatened the entire future of California's coastal redwood forests.

The early twentieth century marked the apex of San Francisco's Gilded Age, which converged with the golden age of opera. Several prominent San Franciscans in the Big Basin campaign—among them Will Hearst and Timothy Hopkins—were ardent supporters of the San Francisco Opera, where Jennie Jeter was a regular patron.

San Francisco, hungering to see the greatest artists perform, invited the Metropolitan Opera to send some of its most illustrious members on tour in 1906. Enrico Caruso, the famous tenor, sang Don José in Bizet's *Carmen* on the night of April 17.[110] The new opera house had electric lights, adding to the already dazzling array of patrons. High society matrons and their daughters in satin and chiffon gowns were amply rewarded by the local papers providing detailed descriptions of their ermine wraps and diamond chokers. Subsequently, the evening would be called the greatest display of wealth in the city's history.[111] Nonetheless, forty-eight hours later, some of the patrons would be among those standing in food lines.

It was near midnight when Jennie Jeter and a friend left the Opera House and returned to their room at the iconic Palace Hotel, where Caruso also stayed. He recalled waking up around 5:00 a.m. feeling his bed rocking like a ship on the ocean; it was, in fact, a massive 7.7 to 8.3 magnitude earthquake.[112]

Jennie Jeter used these opera glasses at the performance of *Carmen* at San Francisco's Grand Opera House. The following morning, April 18, 1906, the building's roof completely collapsed along with thousands of other buildings. *Author's Collection.*

The tenor heard the nonstop sound of masonry crashing amid terror-filled cries as his valet apparently helped him dress. (He later denied press reports that he fled in hysteria with a fur coat over his pajamas and a wet towel protecting his throat.) Caruso, Jennie and the other guests, together with the staff, all made it out safely. But the supposedly fireproof hotel—the most frequently used venue by Big Basin advocates and long-term residence of land scrip speculator William Chapman—went up in flames.

The fires that engulfed the city forced hundreds of thousands of residents to live in tents in Golden Gate Park. The unimaginable catastrophe precipitated a deep but short-lived depression.[113] San Francisco had to replace thirty thousand structures in record time. During the damage assessment, a vital fact emerged: the resilience of the coastal redwoods.

Buildings with redwood façades had served as firewalls, proving there could be no better material for the city's reconstruction. Within weeks, the building industry touted the wonders of redwood lumber.[114] The logging interests claimed that were it not for the use of redwood as the

This page: The post-earthquake disaster documentation in 1906 made use of an innovative technique: photography. These photos of redwood frame buildings still standing created a stampede for the fire-retardant qualities of coastal redwood. *Courtesy of Forest History Society, Durham, North Carolina.*

insulating material between buildings, the inferno would have caused even greater damage. The city required that every new structure be constructed with metal, redwood or stone, and in 1906, fifty-five million more feet of redwood were used than in 1905.[115]

Early estimates said two billion board feet would be needed, but badly damaged San Francisco lumber yards had only fifty million board feet in stock. American lumbering had never experienced such intensity. The record-breaking year involved not just the output of lumber but also the priced charged. The skyrocketing demand brought with it a host of problems, primarily price gouging with claims that the lumber dealers' profits were up more than 500 percent. The Southern Pacific faced a major fiasco. Thousands of railroad cars backed up on its tracks when consignees refused to unload.[116]

In San Jose—also hard-hit by the earthquake—tragedies for the Sempervirens Club stalwarts mounted. When the Dougherty building in downtown San Jose burned to the ground, A.P. Hill's entire collection of negatives, including hundreds of views of Big Basin, went up in flames. The award-winning artist lost twenty-four thousand negatives and all of

Inside A.P. Hill's studio, located in San Jose's Dougherty Building, Florence Hill sat among the many examples of her husband's versatile talent, all of which were destroyed. *Courtesy of Sourisseau Academy, SJSU.*

111 Dougherty Building, Second St., San Jose, Cal. After the Earthquake, Apr. 18, 1906.

When A.P. Hill's studio was demolished by the 1906 earthquake and subsequent fire, his lifetime of work and all his equipment were lost. *Sourisseau Academy SJSU*.

his equipment. Hill said goodbye, at least temporarily, to his decades-long career. He took up gold mining in Fresno and, according to the *Sentinel*, "was as enthusiastic over his gold quartz as he was over the Santa Cruz giant redwoods."[117] Nonetheless, however much time he may have spent in Fresno, his home base remained San Jose, and it wouldn't be long before he was once again advocating for the Big Basin redwoods.

Carrie Walter had only recently become a full-time editor for the newly created *San Jose Times*, a demanding job under any circumstances but more so during the greatest urban disaster in American history. Her heartbreak had to be severe seeing the ruins of Santa Clara County historic structures she had painstakingly promoted. How would the woman who had done the most to publicize in print the Big Basin campaign be remembered when she passed away in 1907?

She received a moving tribute from the Sempervirens Club honoring her dedication to Big Basin. In reporting on her death, a Santa Cruz paper briefly acknowledged Carrie Stevens Walter in conjunction with the park's creation but not so with the widely read *San Jose Evening News*. The obituary lauded her abilities as a writer, poet and newspaperwoman and her statewide renown but omitted a single mention of her championing the Sempervirens' cause.[118] With the club's most eloquent voice now gone, would this be the moment when women began to be erased from the story?

Moreover, with the loss of Walter and Hill dealing with the tragic destruction of his life's work, where did that leave the Sempervirens at such a precarious moment? Though membership was listed as 439, less than half (179) were in good standing. All of the club's scrapbooks, diligently complied by W.W. Richards, burned in the post-earthquake fire.

Five months after the earthquake, the newly completed Big Basin Road opened to the public. Had it been any other year, the major change at Big Basin would have garnered considerable attention and certainly a Sempervirens Club celebration. Local news reported that Will and Jennie Jeter, together with their neighbors the Demings, were among the first Santa Cruzans to drive the inviting mountain thoroughfare from Boulder Creek (today's Highway 236). As exhilarating as it must have felt, the frenzied state of redwood logging made the Jeters' goal of "access for all" fraught with peril.

RAPE OF THE REDWOODS

Republican supporters of the Southern Pacific made certain Governor Pardee served only one term. By championing policies to conserve natural resources, consistent with President Roosevelt's vision, Pardee had done himself in. Had he remained in office beyond 1906, what ensued—whether a deliberate scheme or complete incompetence—would probably have been avoided. During the Big Basin fire of 1904 and the catastrophic fires following the 1906 earthquake, Pardee's skilled management of Sacramento's response deserved more acknowledgement than it got.

The new Republican governor, James Gillet, also head of the state forestry board, enjoyed strong support from the railroad industry. He fired park warden Pilkington and replaced him with a former state senator, Samuel Rambo of Boulder Creek. The first warden's loyalty had been to the park. In a few short years, he had established both a telephone and mail system and actively discouraged visitors from putting any signs or name cards on the trees. Rambo, his successor, had close ties to the Southern Pacific. With his motto of "park improvement," Rambo expanded facilities for tourists, putting in cabins, a lodge and sanitary systems while extensively clearing underbrush.

Meanwhile, Josephine McCrackin had relocated to Santa Cruz after the death of her husband. Now in her sixties, she needed a full-time job and found it as a *Sentinel* reporter. Maintaining her environmental activism, she founded the Ladies Forest and Songbird Protective Association (LPFSPA)

Above: Humphrey Pilkington (circa 1909), replaced as Big Basin's first warden, continued his passion for collecting Native American artifacts. In 1929, he donated the entire collection to the City of Santa Cruz. *Courtesy of Natural Resources and Public Health Library, University of California, Berkeley.*

Left: As park warden, S.H. Rambo received the same $1,500 annual salary as his hands-on predecessor Humphrey Pilkington. Yet the new warden, whose business advertisement is featured, spent only a few hours a week at Big Basin. *Courtesy of Ronnie Trubeck Collection.*

Park warden S.H. Rambo had these buildings installed at the Sempervirens Camp. His aggressive expansion of park facilities happened concurrently with the "rape of the Redwoods." *Courtesy of Ronnie Trubeck Collection.*

and included influential local leaders like her boss, McPherson and Jeter as honorary members.

Responding to distressing news about Warden Rambo's improvement plans, she sent him a petition on behalf of the LPFSPA: "We have learned that it is your intention to clear away all underbrush and to take up the old fallen logs on the entire territory, which would give the place the appearance of a city park and destroy the original grandeur of that part of the Big Basin for which we fought so hard to call our own."[119] His response, in the summer of 1907, was a short but reassuring note that her concerns were unfounded.

After the park closed for the winter, Josephine picked up on local rumors that the "clearing" at the park went well beyond just underbrush. Under the supervision of State Forester Lull, a recent arrival in California with no specific knowledge of redwoods, Rambo hired local woodmen to fell standing trees damaged in the 1904 fire. The trees, far from dead, were quite valuable as lumber.

The Sempervirens dispatched an observer to the scene whose dire report infuriated those who had believed that the forest would be preserved in its primeval state. Friendly newspapers jumped in, denouncing the cutting. Josephine McCrackin used the *Sentinel* to urge protests: "God Save the

Redwoods from the State Forester Lull, and the woodman's ax."[120] Unlike 1900, this time, not only did she sign her name but her plea also went statewide. Concerned citizens held "indignation meetings" in Boulder Creek, Santa Cruz, San Jose, Palo Alto, Watsonville and elsewhere during February 1908.[121]

Meanwhile, the scale of the "atrocity" included converting the Sempervirens Camp into a woodyard for slaughtered trees, including "redwoods with the green limbs still attached." A shocked Middleton called the harvesting "legalized vandalism."[122] Reacting to vehement protests from San Jose and Santa Cruz, the governor sent a forestry commission member along with Forester Lull to meet a delegation of Sempervirens at Big Basin. "It is simply a case of the Sempervirens Club claiming that it knows more about forestry than does the department," a contemptuous Lull told the *Sacramento Bee*.[123]

With Dudley as their expert guide, both sides participated in a close inspection, which only added to the preservationists' ire. At the end of the day, the group convened at Middleton's Commercial Hotel in Boulder Creek, where the heated discussion continued. Though the attending commissioner finally agreed to suspend the redwood cutting until further notice, the wary activists maintained their vigilance—with good reason.

For example, the Hollow Tree had been one of the Sempervirens' favorite conifers for which they had searched diligently during the 1901 camping trip. But even with Middleton's assistance, it remained hidden amid the overgrowth. Finally, two persistent explorers—Herbert Jones, Louise's twenty-one-year-old son, and Congregational minister H.M. Tenney—discovered the tree. Years later, Jones reported that the exceptional tree was among those cut down by Rambo's team.

In March 1908, members of the original campaign—Jeter, Hill, Kenna, Louise Jones and several others—met with Dudley at Stanford to solidify their strategy for resolving the controversy. Later that day, during the official meeting on campus, the professor told the forestry commissioners, "We were to keep this park for the sake of the trees as long as they shall live and to leave the reserve in its pristine beauty. It is my contention that the redwood will almost invariably recover if given time, and I believe that many of those cut down in the Basin would have done so."[124]

Dudley provided evidence: photographs of redwoods "apparently burned beyond recovery" sprouting new growth. After several hours of mostly acrimonious discussion, the commission informed the Sempervirens members that they had already decided two weeks earlier not to cut another tree. But the media didn't buy the face-saving ploy, instead providing the public with a triumphant headline: "Big Basin safe from axes. Committee

Herbert Jones (twenty-one) and Reverend H. Melville Tenney showed off the Hollow Tree, which was one of many living trees cut down during the "rape of the Redwoods" ordeal. *Courtesy of Ross Eric Gibson Collection.*

from Sempervirens Club wins complete victory at Stanford. State forestry board promises that no more redwoods will be cut."[125]

The words Dudley used with the forestry commissioners—"leave the reserve in its pristine beauty"—are significant for understanding the terminology of his time. Those involved in the movement consistently described their effort as preservation, and Dudley provided the definition. But it did not mean an area protected from use, clearly shown by the Sempervirens' and Sierra Club's camping trips.

Coincidently, the same year California's forestry board backed off cutting living trees, President Roosevelt appointed the National Conservation Commission, on which former Governor Pardee would serve. As the term *conservation* began to gain traction, Pardee offered his definition: "The use of natural resources at such times, in such quantities, under such circumstances as the needs of the people, their original owners and donors, may require, but without unnecessary waste or destruction and without private monopoly of them."[126]

STABILITY AT LAST

During the "rape of the redwoods" incident, A.P. Hill was back in action. He became the fourth Sempervirens president, a salaried position he held until he passed on in 1922. For the next five years, he led a contentious battle to secure state funding for the Saratoga–Big Basin Road. Santa Cruz leaders Jeter and McPherson joined the campaign while other prominent locals adamantly opposed the idea. When Herbert Jones became the state senator from the Santa Clara region in July 1913, his influence helped turn the tide. Meanwhile, Harry Cowell, who now managed the extensive Cowell family holdings, agreed to sell a piece of Santa Cruz County timberland that was essential for the road. If initially reluctant, Cowell now showed his support for the Sempervirens road campaign and made a $500 donation to the club.

In July 1914, A.P. Hill, Will Jeter and Josephine McCrackin welcomed a crowd gathered for the groundbreaking ceremony at the summit of the Santa Cruz Mountains—at long last a scenic road directly connected Big Basin with Bay Area counties.[127] The road was a major triumph for Hill and his tenacity. Going forward, he could give more time to managing the Ingomer Consolidated Gold Company in Calaveras County, of which he had become the president in 1910, "but it never brought Hill the financial success he had hoped for."[128]

Also in 1910, the profound impact of the "rape of the redwoods" lingered; the public, especially in Santa Cruz County, had legitimate concerns about park management. If the state forester did not know the difference between

Near the Summit, Saratoga Road. Calif. Redwood Park.

William Jeter, chairman of the Good Roads Movement, promoted the Saratoga Road while other powerful Santa Cruzans opposed it for years. With direct access from the Bay Area, they feared the loss of tourism in the city of Santa Cruz. *Courtesy of Sourisseau Academy SJSU.*

a dead redwood and one still living, what else had been neglected under inept state management? Adding insult to injury, Sacramento had made *no attempt* to put safeguards in place to prevent future abuse.

The public needed reminding of the recreational and salubrious value of the Santa Cruz Mountain redwoods, and Jennie Jeter believed it could be accomplished with the right kind of event. Working with her brother Frank Bliss (the author's great-grandfather), a leader of the Santa Cruz Library Board, they decided Santa Cruzans would surely embrace a celebratory day in March 1910. Andrew Carnegie, having achieved the dominant position in the American steel industry by 1900, was often called a robber baron for his labor practices. But in 1901, at age sixty-five, he retired and devoted his remaining years to philanthropy. His support for libraries nationwide included funding for a much-needed Santa Cruz library building. Jennie predicted that a sit-down steak luncheon at Big Trees in Felton, after a tour of the library, would help pay tribute to Carnegie's generosity and also make good headlines for the trees.

The warm gentleman showed irrepressible delight over the conifers and wished he could stay for a month.[129] A.A. Taylor explained to him "that the Mariposa Grove may contain trees of a greater circumference but the local

Above: Andrew Carnegie's visit to Santa Cruz in 1910 recaptured positive media attention for the old-growth redwoods. An Associated Press story—carried in several papers—told of the family's joy-filled day at the trees. *Courtesy of Santa Cruz Public Library*.

Right: Elizabeth Richards, wife of sportsman W.W. Richards, had a relaxing day of fishing at Big Basin, circa 1910. Grizzly bears roamed the park hunting for fish until the late 1800s, and the area's pioneers enjoyed steelhead trout as a regular part of their diet. *Courtesy of History San Jose*.

grove contained the highest redwood tree known. Mr. Carnegie was very much pleased to know that Santa Cruz had the highest trees as he was for Santa Cruz first and last, all the time." His wife, Louise, especially taken with the efforts of Jennie's décor committee, commented to the women: "That's the happy way to live, to be able to get along without servants as much as possible. You Western people take the initiative, and do not helplessly depend upon others to wait upon you."[130]

Local media celebrated the day as one of the happiest events in the history of Santa Cruz. The *Call* sent its own photographer from San Francisco, and major papers throughout the state ran the Associated Press story of the philanthropist's visit. A touch of irony perhaps was that the reporter mistakenly referred to the location as Big Basin instead of Big Trees. Regardless, the awe-inspiring beauty and sublimity of the coastal redwoods were very much in the news once again.

A Clean Sweep and a Sad Goodbye

Meanwhile in Sacramento, first-term State Senator James Holohan from Santa Cruz's South County had led the charge to safeguard the park against future plunder of the people's trees. His bill, supported by the Sempervirens, would remove management of Big Basin from the Forestry Bureau and place it in the hands of a non-political commission. But Governor Gillet, in cahoots with the Southern Pacific, vetoed the bill, claiming, "The damage is done and there is no likelihood of any such damage occurring again."[131]

Father Kenna adamantly disagreed. In August, he reentered the fray by way of a lengthy letter to the *Sacramento Bee*, reprinted in several other papers. His exhortation was well timed to provide context and support for gubernatorial candidate Hiram Johnson, a progressive Republican and good friend. Kenna explained the core values of those who began the movement, adding his own coda, "To save the trees for posterity: to save the trees for scientific study and also many species of Fauna, in the basin, and…to form a great park for the people…whither our children and workmen factory girls and others breathing all week impure air, might amidst the great trees and along rippling Brooks breathe pure air, where their minds and hearts are lifted to hire pure nobler things."[132]

He implored the Sempervirens "to renew an ever-increasing energy for the salvation of the trees and the development and opening of the park and to avoid those expressions which caused many people to say the club acts and speaks as if the Big Basin belonged to it and they alone had the whole say concerning it."[133]

Hiram Johnson's November victory propelled a new direction in California politics. His anti–Southern Pacific platform allied him with Jeter, Delmas and other prominent Democrats who had long fought the anti-monopoly battle. At the start of the 1911 legislative session, Senator Holohan reintroduced his bill to put management of Big Basin back under the auspices of commissioners.[134] Five weeks later, Governor Johnson announced his appointments—unpaid positions—to the California Redwood Park Commission.

Santa Cruz County, snubbed in 1902 when the original commission by the same name was appointed, now had two commissioners. With A.A. Taylor as one of the them, the *Sentinel* was rapturous about a former rival. The paper offered effusive details about the editor's extensive knowledge and dedication.[135] And what a vindication for Henry Middleton, who had endured baseless attacks on his character. As a commissioner, the soft-spoken Boulder Creek lumberman would now help oversee the land he had so generously stewarded until the first warden took over in 1903. Both men's prominence in the Democratic Party showed the Republican governor's commitment to expertise over partisanship.

Josephine McCrackin's witty article saluted the new governor for his wise choices. "No more heartaches now and heartbreaks over trees brought to the dust in the spirit of commercialism.…Long-live Governor Johnson and by the way is he Democrat or Republican?" She was every bit as pleased with his other choices: Professor Charles B. Wing of the Stanford engineering department and Father Kenna.[136]

As soon as the new park commission was legally established, Governor Johnson persuaded the ailing priest to be his first appointment. However frail, Father Kenna's participation sent a vital message of unrelenting commitment. He had helped found the movement at Stanford on May 1, 1900, when Dudley's extensive research revealed imminent danger to Big Basin.

When Professor Dudley began his systematic study of Big Basin's botany in the early 1890s, he and Captain Clarke, working for the *Surf*, were the only ones known to be collecting data and taking photographs of the region. Now on his deathbed, he could take satisfaction in all that had been accomplished. Just a few weeks before Dudley's passing in 1911, the new group of commissioners removed Warden Rambo and his deputy from all responsibilities at Big Basin.[137] At last, after a tortuous time, the park was in safe hands.

In 1909, Santa Cruzans came together to provide a permanent home for their revered local journalist Josephine McCrackin. She lived and wrote at 331 Pacheco Street, Santa Cruz, for the next decade. *Courtesy of Santa Cruz MAH.*

Beloved by Stanford students, the botanist Dudley left no immediate family; instead, his legacy was an incomparable forest. Perhaps his genteel modesty contributed to insufficient recognition for his commitment to data-driven activism. In his memoir, Stanford president David Starr Jordan pointed out his own role in convincing Governor Gage to sign the California Redwood Park Bill but only mentioned Dudley in passing, as part of a list of those who had lobbied for it.[138] Ninety years after his death, his significant contribution finally began receiving the acknowledgement it deserved.[139]

Father Kenna died the following year. Governor Johnson wrote a moving tribute: "He it was who saved for the state the California Redwood Park." Noting the priest's abounding love of nature, Johnson said that his friend's "final words included his plans for protection and preservation of the trees." The *Sacramento Bee* described his most important plan as ensuring "that the trees will remain forever the heritage particularly of the poor and their children."[140]

Father Kenna, from his earliest involvement, saw Big Basin as "a breathing place for the people." After a tumultuous decade, that vision of the possible would begin to be realized. With the same focus and devotion, the boy from Mississippi who lost his mother at age five also secured the future of his

Left: For two decades, Professor William Dudley inspired Stanford students with his activism to preserve and protect Big Basin in its natural state. *Courtesy of Special Collections Stanford.*

Below: Father Robert Kenna's (*center top*) lifetime of service to others included his support for every aspect of student life at Santa Clara College. He twice served as the college president. *Courtesy of Special Collections SCU.*

The Saratoga–Big Basin Road provided Bay Area communities with far easier access to the park. The entrance sign had been changed from State Redwood Park to read California Redwood Park. *Courtesy of Frank Perry Collection.*

institution. Just weeks after Kenna's death in 1912, Santa Clara College officially became Santa Clara University.

With the opening of the Saratoga–Big Basin Road in 1915, some of the scenes for a daring Hollywood movie were filmed at Big Basin. Given that the park's land had been first acquired through scrip belonging to "half-breed" Dakota, how ironic that the film was titled *Half-Breed*. Douglas Fairbanks, with his signature athleticism, plays the protagonist, Lo Dorman. "It is essentially a story condemning racism and hypocrisy," said a film critic who noted Fairbanks's later reflection: "We, who had a hand in making it, regarded it as a knockout….But the public, again using the more expressive vernacular, couldn't see it."[141]

Visitors continued flocking to the free paradise each year and persisted in calling it Big Basin despite its official name: California Redwood Park. The creation of the state park system in 1927 brought with it a new and permanent name: Big Basin Redwoods State Park, where everyone is "privileged to come and spend the day."

10

THE LAST CAMPAIGN FOR
THE MOUNTAIN REDWOODS

*For many nineteenth- and early twentieth-century residents of Santa
Cruz County, the mountain redwoods were woven into the fabric of their
lives—not so much as separate and distinct forests but as one pervasive
landscape, as it had once been for the Indigenous people. Whatever old-
growth* Sequoia sempervirens *remained, they, too, deserved to be saved.*

In contrast to the state's successful stewardship at Big Basin, the owners
of Big Trees Grove in Felton had not upgraded any buildings, and
evidently did not provide bathrooms for paying customers. Nonetheless,
the four Welch heirs had doubled their admission fees from a quarter to fifty
cents by 1921, which a guard dutifully collected. Even the public outrage
and strongly worded objection by Santa Cruz mayor Carl Katzenstein had
no effect.[142]

Ever since he had courted Jennie in the 1880s, Jeter had promised
that one day Big Trees Grove would be a public park.[143] But who would
compose the team of activists now? By the early 1920s, most members of
the original movement had passed on: Dudley, Hill, Kenna, Kron, Phoebe
Hearst, McCrackin, McPherson, Smith and Walter, with Middleton mostly
incapacitated from a stroke. Will and Jennie Jeter maintained their friendship
with a few founding members of the Sempervirens, especially Louise Jones,
who continued to live in San Jose. But it would require a cohesive group of
Santa Cruzans to move the Grove from private to public ownership.

During the 1920s, Jennie and Will Jeter (*couple, upper left*) organized Beach Hill neighbors for Sunday drives to Big Basin. Included here are Henry Deming (*lower right*) and his wife, Josephine (*upper left*). *Courtesy of Special Collections UCSC.*

Jeter, newspaperman H.R. Judah and other local businessmen founded the Santa Cruz Rotary Club in 1922. Well suited to promote a county-owned redwood park, the nascent club embraced the environmental cause. Soon after its first meeting in March, the club invited Rotary International—which would be convening in Los Angeles in June—to visit the Big Trees Grove. Nearly four hundred Rotarians from several states and thirty-four countries made the Santa Cruz Mountain redwoods their destination heading home from the convention.

When the awestruck men, committed to humanitarian goals, marveled at the massive trees in the cool forest air, the local press went wild with hyperbole: "Never again can Santa Cruz hope to be host to such a cosmopolitan gathering." Rotary International second vice president, Mr. Alexander Wilkie of Scotland, referred to the Big Trees Grove as nature's temple of God and the redwood itself as almost immortal: "I can conceive of no truer emblem of the spirit of Rotary....It symbolizes life everlasting, work

The "Giant"

Opposite: In 1922, Rotarians from throughout the world gathered around the Giant Tree at Welch's Big Trees Grove. In June 1938, five hundred members from dozens of clubs dedicated the tree to Rotary International. *Courtesy of Special Collections UCSC.*

Right: A.A. Taylor's gravestone, a prominent marker immediately inside the entrance of Evergreen Cemetery, includes this commemorative plaque. For forty years, the newspaperman informed Santa Cruzans about Big Basin. *Photo by Gary Neier.*

and human effort everlasting for the good of the world, and this is the true spirit of Rotary." The international audience—including representatives from Uruguay, South America, Ireland, London and France—provided an illustrious and rousing soft launch for a second redwood park campaign.[144]

But the following year, Will Jeter felt a keen loss with the passing of A.A. Taylor. During his six years serving as a state redwood park commissioner and the commission's secretary (1911–17), he had developed the process whereby the state could acquire highly desirable private land adjacent to Big Basin. His foresight helped make possible the park's eventual expansion to eighteen thousand acres, five times the original size. On the second anniversary of his death, August 1925, a crowd gathered around the Taylor family plot at Santa Cruz's Evergreen Cemetery to honor the unrelenting reformer. Jeter read aloud from the memorial plaque donated by the community."[145] Whenever duty called, Taylor had stepped up and for no cause more tenaciously than Big Basin.[146]

Two events in 1926 indirectly accelerated the Big Trees campaign. In the final weeks of 1925, the Redwood Park Commission went on record in favor of a Big Basin entrance fee. Jeter, the first to jump on the news, used his leadership position with the Santa Cruz Chamber of Commerce to express their collective "repulsion" over the unthinkable idea.[147] To mobilize against the plan, he presided at the annual meeting of the Sempervirens

Club in San Jose and invited local influencers to join him: the editors of the *Sentinel* and the *Mountain Echo*. Their wives joined Jennie Jeter at the event, determined to reaffirm the park's free access.

Was Big Basin really about to join Big Trees in charging admission? Imagine the outrage! State Senator Herbert Jones of San Jose, consulting lawyer for the Sempervirens Club, "roundly condemned" the proposed fee. His motion that vehemently reasserted "the principle of maintaining a virgin park free to all" received unanimous support from the members.[148] Chambers of commerce throughout the region supported the Sempervirens' protest, proving the club of forest advocates still had clout a quarter century after its founding.

In early April 1926, the Redwood Park Commission voted: no fee of any kind except for camping privileges. Jeter's friend, fellow Rotarian and newspaper editor H. R. Judah, reiterated community values in an editorial: "The park belongs to the people of the state, and such property can be used by the nature lover, the tired businessman, the budding lovers, the happy rollicking family in a Ford and all other groups of the great American human melting pot as a delightful place of relaxation and at any and all times without charge."[149] The idea of charging admission seemed so contrary to the park ideal that the next Big Basin brochure published in Santa Cruz proclaimed: "The park is absolutely free."

The well-timed victory coincided with a radical change in the Welch family dynamics. With the death of his older brother, Herman, Joseph Jr. inherited his quarter share in the Big Trees Land and Development Company, incorporated in 1902. Now with the controlling interest, he could speak persuasively on the family's behalf. Having spent his career living in Los Angeles, he had avoided some of the local animosity toward his brothers and their rising entrance fees. To further his parents' preservationist goals, Welch wanted Big Trees Grove to be a local park and enlisted Jeter to help pursue a deal with the county. But complex and cumbersome negotiations dragged on as months turned into years.

In 1928, Santa Cruz Rotary provided the ideal opportunity for Jeter to pressure the county supervisors into action. To a packed house of Rotarians and their guests, he presented the map of the Grove's forty acres of old-growth redwoods and introduced Joseph Welch Jr. as his oldest friend.[150] To those, including Jennie, who had decried Stanly Welch's fence, an uncommonly blunt Jeter had this to say: "That huge fence around the trees that has caused so much criticism made this preservation possible."[151]

Senator Herbert Jones, at the state capitol in 1923, adhered to his Quaker upbringing throughout his life. He maintained the Sempervirens Club— his mother, Louise's, legacy—for several decades. *Courtesy Jones Family Collection.*

In Big Basin's early decades, families settled in at the park, often camping for weeks at a time. *Courtesy of Ross Eric Gibson Collection.*

Above: In the 1920s, drivers parked immediately adjacent to Big Basin's trees. This practice compacted the understory, preventing adequate aeration for the redwoods' shallow root system. *Courtesy of Ronnie Trubeck Collection.*

Left: Cecil B. DeMille filmed *Romance of the Redwoods* staring Mary Pickford (1917) at Big Trees Grove. By the mid-1920s, the carelessness of some other film companies caused visible damage to the trees. *Author's Collection.*

Rotarians flexed their collective muscle. Within a month, the supervisors had a motion for purchase on the table, but they had concerns about Welch's specific restrictions. Big Basin suffered from automobiles; cars parked far too close to the trees harmed their understory. Joseph Jr. would not repeat that mistake. Close proximity of vehicles to the Grove's giants was unacceptable; unless the county agreed to a reasonable distance between all parking and the Grove itself, there would be no deal.

Jeter—trying to craft a solution—was blindsided when the supervisors received a competing plan for the Grove's future. Mr. Bedford, a Hollywood developer, made an enticing pitch. Big-name stars like Mary Pickford and William S. Hart had thoroughly enjoyed making movies in the redwoods,[152] and Bedford's proposal would help create a movie-making hub. His outfit would buy the entire 365 acres of Welch land with a county park at the center; on the northwest side he would construct a number of single-family homes. It would be an economic boon for the town of Felton and the entire San Lorenzo Valley. But didn't residents understand the harmful long-term impact of a housing development immediately adjacent to the ancient trees? Evidently not. Charged with making a recommendation to the supervisors between the two competing plans, a citizens committee voted seven to three in favor of the developer.

THE FINAL PUSH

To regain momentum, Jeter began a massive public relations campaign speaking to whatever group would listen and writing lengthy explanations of his proposal for the press. But his ponderous prose failed to inspire locals. Deal making was his forte, however, and he succeeded in convincing the Welch family to sweeten the pot for the county by adding more acreage and reducing their asking price from $200,000 to $150,000.

Meanwhile, Jennie had growing concern over Will's declining health amid multiple commitments.[153] In addition to the campaign and serving as full-time County Bank president at age seventy-nine, he chaired the Highways Committee responsible for the creation of the soon-to-be completed Skyline Boulevard. In July 1929, she arranged a trip to Yosemite National Park so that Will could experience firsthand what had been accomplished in the heart of the Valley. Stephen Mather of the Park Service had overcome huge obstacles to open the one-of-a kind Ahwahnee Hotel, built by the architect commissioned for Bryce Canyon and Zion National Parks.

Initially, the Jeters' stay rejuvenated Will just as Jennie had intended. Walking around the outside of the famous hotel, the couple enjoyed awe-inspiring views of Half Dome and Yosemite Falls with their towering granite walls. But, as fate would have it, Jeter's bear encounter became one of the park's most newsworthy events that July. The *Evening News* reported that one of the bears in the park, considered dangerous with a "mean disposition," attacked him on the leg. He fended him off long enough for a nearby ranger to shoot the troublesome animal, allowing Jeter to walk away unscathed.[154] Whether Will received the diagnosis of terminal stomach cancer before or after the Yosemite trip is unknown.

In September 1929, the supervisors responded to questioning by the Jeters' close friend Milo Hopkins, who operated a successful concession adjacent to the Welchs' Grove. He wanted to know the extent of their commitment. The board agreed it would not go back on its resolution: $75,000 allocated for the Welch land with the other $75,000 to be raised by Jeter. But it still would not accept the parking restrictions insisted upon by Welch. Moreover, how could Jeter quickly raise such a sum with his health deteriorating? Those worries were in abeyance for a short time when he got a much-needed boost—the opening of the majestic Skyline Boulevard, Jeter's career-long dream. The press reports emphasized it was "a new through connection between San Francisco Peninsula points and the Big Basin, Santa Cruz, Watsonville, or points on the Monterey Peninsula."[155]

Barely two weeks later, on October 11, the country turned upside-down when the stock market crashed. Jeter, with waning energy, focused on the stability of the County Bank. Throughout their marriage, Jeter had engineered Jennie's fight for accessible trees while she remained the "good wife" whose public activities stayed within proper social constraints. Now she had to take charge and somehow raise the additional $75,000 despite the looming Depression. Together they managed to get buy-in from Southern Pacific Railroad, Crocker Bank and a few locals, including Milo Hopkins. But where could she turn for the additional $50,000 still needed?

Save the Redwoods League (SRL) seemed like a good prospect. Will respected Director Newton B. Drury and no doubt admired the SRL lobbying effort that had succeeded in creating the State Parks Commission in 1927. Composed mostly of eastern Republican men, SRL had been enormously successful with fundraising and by 1928 had raised over half a million dollars to acquire three thousand acres of redwood forest. Though a potential donor, Jennie opposed any help from those committed to eugenics, which included at least eleven of the leading men in the league.

For the *Overland Monthly*, Josephine McCrackin wrote about the unique features of the Jeters' Cliff Crest home at 407 Cliff Street, Santa Cruz, especially the expansive garden with its thriving redwoods. *Courtesy of Santa Cruz Public Library*.

SRL founder Madison Grant achieved considerable renown as the author of the bestselling book *Passing of the Great Race*, published in 1916. "He was as personable in social settings as he was savage in his pursuit of an ethnically pristine America."[156] What exactly did "ethnically pristine" mean in the 1920s? "They supported selective breeding, through which superior Aryans would gradually weed out inferior strains."[157] For Jennie, that commitment to a so-called pure, uncontaminated race was anathema to the message of redwood parks, not to mention her strong abolitionist roots. The beckoning of the world's trees was to provide welcoming solace and regeneration for one and all.

Yet Jennie had to secure the Grove while Will was alive to see it happen. After his brief hospital stay, she turned Cliff Crest, their Beach Hill home,

The first member of the Sempervirens Club to "discover" Big Basin was Louise Jones, who wrote about being enamored with the redwood forest in 1872. *Courtesy of Jones Family Collection.*

into a perpetual open house. Assisted by a cadre of Rotary Club members, she invited Santa Cruzans "to stop in and bid farewell any afternoon." Hundreds came and kept coming. Did they come to say goodbye to the man who gave his all protecting their trees? Probably not. To them, he was the bank president who, for thirty-seven years, had warmly welcomed each customer who walked through the door.

Of the countless favors Will had done others, his character was never to call one in. Under the circumstances, Jennie had no such reservations. When a visitor would ask, "What can I do?" she urged, "Make sure your supervisor doesn't change his commitment to a park because of dwindling county funds." Of the many calls Jennie made on Will's behalf that year, the most important was to Joseph Welch Jr., who arrived from San Francisco in time to say farewell. Welch—Will's friend of fifty years—assured him that he would cover the remaining amount required for the purchase, essentially paying for his own land.

On May 15, Will Jeter passed away at Hanly Hospital knowing that Santa Cruz County Big Trees Park would soon be a reality. In September 1930, the supervisors unanimously accepted his plan, including Welch's restrictions on parking: 120 acres were now owned by the county. That victory gave a capstone to the era of preservation activists. Just a few months before Jeter's passing, Louise Jones of San Jose and Henry Middleton of Boulder Creek—both known for constancy and community-building in their efforts to protect the trees—had been laid to rest.

PERMANENT PROTECTION

For forty years, almost all of those who entered the Grove had paid for the privilege. Beginning in September 1931, everyone could freely enjoy the Big Trees. As the Depression deepened, what better lift for sinking spirits than communing with the redwoods? At the dedication of the Jeter Tree in 1934, Jennie held a reception at the park to thank hundreds of Santa Cruzans who had made it possible.[158]

At last, the Santa Cruz Mountains had two public parks to protect the redwoods in perpetuity. But were they really protected? The post–World

Santa Cruz County Big Trees Park served nature lovers for more than twenty years. In the mid-1950s, it became the centerpiece of Henry Cowell Redwoods State Park. *Courtesy of Santa Cruz MAH.*

The Jeter Tree -
Big Trees Park -
Santa Cruz Co., Calif..

9110

Above: In 1946, Big Basin State Park was on the way to becoming a full-service resort, with the installation of a huge swimming pool. *Courtesy of Frank Perry Collection.*

Opposite: For the Jeter Tree at Santa Cruz County Big Trees Park, Jennie Bliss Jeter selected a tree visible from the trail, although today it is harder to recognize. The plaque, long-ago removed from the redwood, was placed close to the trail, not far from the Wonder Tree. *Courtesy of Author's Collection.*

War Two era brought a new kind of tourism to the Santa Cruz Mountains. Far from what the early preservationists envisioned—communing with the redwoods in the most natural setting—the forests now offered resort-like experiences. At Big Basin, the installation of a large swimming pool in 1946 accommodated families eager for more recreational opportunities than the natural ecosystem provided. A 1948 fire in the surrounding area precipitated an official closing of the pool the following year.

At the edge of Santa Cruz County Big Trees Park, performances of extravagant, so-called miracle plays with huge casts of one hundred or more, attracted teeming crowds, often spilling over into the park itself. Thousand-year-old trees served as mere backdrops for the hammy, grandiose shows. As Jennie's disquiet grew over mounting commercialization—a far cry from her concept of universal access—she knew she had to act.

Immediately to the south and west of Santa Cruz County Big Trees Park was a large expanse of land owned by the surviving heirs of Henry Cowell, Harry and Isabella. Neither had children of their own because the

Heir to the Cowell fortune, bachelor Harry Cowell waited until his nineties to make an enduring contribution to the preservation of old-growth redwoods. *Courtesy of Special Collections UCSC.*

patriarch did not want any of his children to marry. Known as California's lime king and timber baron, Henry Cowell "probably cut more San Lorenzo Valley redwoods than anyone else."[159]

In 1950, with the death of his sister, Isabella, Harry (aka Samuel Henry), at age ninety-two, was the last of the Cowell line. Jennie reached out to Harry, who had become her friend through a mutual interest in horseback riding, when she arrived in Santa Cruz. Now, both in their nineties and the last of an entire generation, she hoped he would commit to the long-term survival of Santa Cruz County Big Trees Park.

Jennie's hopes were realized when, in November 1953, Harry's negotiations with the state were consummated. He gave 1,623 acres surrounding the Grove—a type of buffer for the grove of ancient redwoods—in exchange for the entire area becoming a state park and named for his father. "He had been offered big money by lumbering interests for the giant redwoods, but admired their beauty and did not want to see them cut."[160] Nonetheless, by having the county park absorbed in the new state park, the dedicated stewardship of Santa Cruzans was erased.

A half-century earlier, Timothy Hopkins and Henry Middleton, with fathers whose businesses had cut down thousands of acres of redwoods, together made Big Basin Redwoods State Park possible. In the process, they spared no effort or expense to accommodate the Sempervirens' requests. By contrast there is no evidence that Harry Cowell's deal—which redeemed his family name—included any input from county residents whose support had made the original park possible.

Harry Cowell died a few months before the official opening of Henry Cowell Redwoods State Park.[161] Jennie did not attend the event in 1955 but, when asked, provided her buggy for the historical reenactment. She passed on four years later, a few months prior to her 100th birthday.

Today, more than one million visitors a year from all over the world marvel at the sublimity of the primeval forest. Some of them might notice a small plaque mounted on a ground level rock honoring the "unselfish efforts" of William T. Jeter. Of the 2.5 million acres of California's redwood forest that existed two hundred years ago, just 5 percent remain today. What would that number be if it weren't for the heroic woman and men of Big Basin and the Santa Cruz Mountain redwoods?

EPILOGUE

In the summer of 2020, 120 years after the movement to save Big Basin commenced at Stanford University, the park was inundated with visitors—as a Shangri-la type refuge from the unrelenting pandemic—and then suffered an unimaginable catastrophe. The common thread weaving together the past with the present and future is the uncommon commitment of those who love Big Basin.

The Weekend Crowds of July 2020

Cars filled with frustrated families stretched for miles as they waited for parking spaces to free up. The lines were far longer than any ranger had ever seen—visitors desperate to be in Big Basin hailed from two directions: Saratoga to the north and Boulder Creek to the west.

Instead of her usual role of connecting people with the diverse ecosystem, State Parks Interpreter Susan Blake spent the day trying to calm travelers' frayed nerves and assist park staff with the throng. "We all gently suggested visitors come back on a weekday when more parking would be available," she said. "But most of them, having driven so far, wanted to still come in, having waited weeks for the park to reopen from the COVID-19 closure in the spring." Desperate for a restart, Bay Area residents forgot about the profound parking shortage that has plagued Big Basin for a century.[162]

Concurrently, Susan faced another challenge. Volunteer docents had always been in abundant supply on weekends, offering visitors special programs and guided walks. Due to the pandemic, that number had been reduced to just a couple. During her fourteen years as Big Basin's only year-round interpreter, Susan had encountered every type of problem—from helping a group of youngsters who had stepped in a wasp nest to staying up all night in the Sempervirens Room with a mother and children as rescuers searched for her lost husband and son. Yet never before had Susan experienced a severe shortage of energetic volunteers. Training, managing and inspiring forty to fifty docents has always been a calling for Susan. "Nothing is more rewarding than learning the endless lessons nature has to teach and sharing them in fresh, creative ways with our docents and the general public."

The Role of Park Interpreter

When I first met Susan, four years earlier, her job seemed close to idyllic. She invited me to give my *Saving Big Basin* talk to several dozen docents and a handful of park rangers. Although I had presented the topic to receptive Santa Cruz and Silicon Valley organizations as well as to my fellow docents at Henry Cowell Redwoods State Park, I felt nervous with this group, unsure of what to expect.

They had been infused with the story of one heroic male, A.P. Hill, as the discoverer and savior of the park. With a proliferation of books, brochures and park memorials—some more than a century old—the dramatic legend was etched into memory. For example, in the State Parks' 2011 Big Basin brochure, Hill was referred to six times, but no other person, man or woman, received any mention. When I asked about the "misinformation by omission," I was told by a park supervisor that "history is much easier for the public to grasp when it is about a single individual." But at the highest echelon, I got a much different response. John Laird, then California's secretary of natural resources, encouraged me to pursue a complete history that celebrated the extraordinary team effort.

Earlier that year, 2016, I spent several hours with a prominent docent who had dedicated himself to Hill and the "one-great-man legend." He was quite antagonistic over my having collaborated with a State Parks staff member. What was the ruckus all about? I had been asked as a volunteer to revise the 2011 brochure to reflect more of the true Big Basin story based on a journal

In 2017, characterizing the team spirit of Big Basin, Mountain Parks Foundation provided this electric bike for Interpreter Susan Blake, and docent Bill Rhoades assembled it. The new mobility enabled her to have more frequent contact with each campground. *Courtesy of Bill Rhoades Collection.*

article I had recently coauthored.[163] For example, the old brochure said, "In 1900, Hill gathered many staunch supporters to tour the area." For the 2015 brochure, I replaced that with the verified account: "After a landmark meeting at Stanford University in May of 1900, Santa Cruz businessmen led Hill, journalists, and politicians on an excursion to Big Basin." The docent was even more infuriated that I had quoted Carrie Stevens Walter in the revised brochure—the first time she's ever been acknowledged in one. The docent's upset seemed completely out of proportion. The staff member and I had made some progress with accuracy, but Hill still dominated the revised brochure (2015) with six mentions and a self-portrait. No one else in the movement was pictured though I had provided appropriate photos.

The twenty or so docents who came for my talk—held in the Lodge at Big Basin—seemed genuinely engaged and appreciated historic photos they hadn't seen before. I looked forward to their questions. But that allotted time turned out to be an unexpected declaration of differences. The infuriated docent, who enjoyed a following among some in the group, displayed his stack of photos one by one, determined to disprove my story and reaffirm the one-hero mythology. His contentiousness made it feel like a courtroom with my narrative being the "witness" under cross-examination.

Two female docents followed me to my car and rather apologetically said they appreciated my much fuller account but didn't feel comfortable saying so publicly. During my hour-drive home to Santa Cruz, I wondered what it would take to unclasp the stranglehold of misinformation.

Two weeks later, I felt a bit relieved hearing from one of the park rangers who had attended the talk. He approached me while we were in line for groceries in Felton and said, "Your research makes sense. It took all kinds of skills to create our first state park and the environmental movement. Rangers think the old guard volunteers should start embracing the role of women."

In 2018, I took a few friends to a Mountain Parks Foundation outdoor event for donors. Our docent for the Big Basin Redwood Loop walk, Hal Anjo, had us enthralled with his tour. In telling the broader story of the park's founding, he emphasized Louise Jones and Carrie Walter, saying, "Everyone had a vital role to play and there was no one hero." Susan, with around fifteen docents, then performed a reenactment of the park's creation in the Campfire Center. A couple of docents asked me afterward if I liked the way they had used my research to enhance their characters and the overall story. *Very much so.* Susan, having given a rich portrayal of Josephine McCrackin herself, later reflected on the gradual change in thinking: "We've all been so used to Hill dominating center stage that your research caused a disconnect. But the disparate threads can all be woven together. He's still very much on the stage, but now has to share the limelight with several other equally important figures."

THE CAMPFIRE CENTER

I had always experienced the Campfire Center—where Susan and the docents had performed on a fantastic stage—as an ideal state park structure. A beckoning amphitheater with a huge brick fire pit and around one hundred benches— each constructed from a redwood—accommodating several hundred people. Moreover, the ambiance felt consistent with the Sempervirens' original goal for the park: "To be preserved in a state of nature."

A few years into her Big Basin life, Susan felt concerned over the diminishing attendance at evening programs in the Campfire Center. Her idea for a different type of fun event for families blossomed:

Once a week in the afternoon, I'd start a blazing fire, put out 100 small apples, and set up a table of amazing skulls and pelts representing animals in the park. My brother, a music lover, created a delightful CD of campfire music. Our backlit movie screen was perfect for shadow puppets which we taped to paint-stir sticks. We had an endless supply of sticks for puppet shows because my teacher dad explained to paint store owners why his daughter needed paint sticks.

Families had a wholesome choice of activities: They could roast apples or marshmallows, earn prizes for answering questions about the skulls and pelts, create stories and plays with the shadow puppets, play bean bag, or just sit happily listening to music in such a beautiful setting. It was my absolute favorite program. I loved to see the joy in the kids' faces, the relaxed look of the parents as they saw their children safely play, and I could answer questions about my favorite place on the planet.

Susan Blake's Roasted Apple Recipe

Select apple and stick it on dowel
Roast over safe campfire until skin is ashy black (four to five minutes)
Peel off skin with paper towel
Roll in cinnamon and sugar
Cook over campfire until sugar caramelizes

When Susan led the final campfire program for the 2019 season, with apple-roasting still the most popular activity, there was no reason to think her unique outdoor life at Big Basin would ever be different. Exactly one year later, that entire world was gone.

The Ashes of 2020

When Susan awoke in the pre-dawn hours of August 16, she was instantly in awe of the sound and beauty of the intense lightning storm. She didn't think of fire as she dressed for work that morning. But on her way to Big Basin Park Headquarters—just three miles away—she could barely see past the swirls of thick smoke. Within a few hours, she and other park staff were given a tall order: complete closure of the six-mile trail to Berry Creek Falls. The COVID-weary visitors who had flocked to the cascading spring that sweltering weekend must now be told to leave.

Monday was relatively uneventful, and Susan remembers that the events of Tuesday, August 18, also felt normal, as Zoom meetings from park headquarters proceeded on schedule. "We knew that multiple fires were burning throughout the county, but none of us had information on fire movement within the park. It was one of the hottest days I can remember; the thermometer registered 100." The lightning strikes had wreaked havoc with hundreds of fires burning throughout California, but Susan and her colleagues had no idea of the enormous strain on the entire Cal Fire system. Nor did they know that a windstorm that afternoon had caused three local fires to merge and significantly expand. The staff's collective mindset seemed like one of general disbelief:

> This is the beloved Big Basin that's endured forever, and we hadn't been told of any imminent danger. That combination made us feel safe. If we'd had any inkling it was roaring toward us, we would have scrambled to save precious artifacts.
>
> By the time I got off work, I could hardly breathe. My husband, Dennis, a manager at Little Basin, was at our new trailer in the area called Upper Meadow, home to several state parks staff. We decided we had to drive out of the San Lorenzo Valley to somewhere we could breathe. I wanted ocean, I wanted cool, fresh air, I wanted to take a breath without having a lung full of smoke. Dennis met me with our dogs, and we headed for Marianne's Ice Cream in Aptos. Finally, refreshing and cool air.
>
> As soon as we got our ice cream cones, we pulled up at Seacliff State Beach. I scrolled through Facebook for fire information and there was a text from our neighbor: "Everyone at both Upper Sky Meadow and Lower Sky Meadow has to evacuate immediately: the fire is here." We couldn't believe it! Right away we sped back over those thirty-two miles to get our cats MelMel and Princessa. Everyone is pouring out of Boulder Creek—a constant stream of headlights coming toward us. Then came law enforcement. On Highway 236, they stopped us, insisting we could not go through unless for family. Of course, cats are family.
>
> As we ran inside the trailer to get them, we noticed a State Parks ranger truck on the road ahead. We heard James Weber and Tyler Knapp yell, "You've got to leave!"

A few months after the 2020 fire, interpreter Susan Blake stood at the steps where the Park Administration Building used to be. These steps are one of the only architectural features that remains from all the historic buildings. *Photo by docent Estrella Bibbey.*

"Just another minute," we yelled back, "we're getting our cats!"
Then James said emphatically, "You've got to get out of here!"
Finally, I said, "Well, where is the fire?"
He pointed just past our lawn. "Right there!"
I was stunned, staring at huge flames only twenty yards away. Dennis got both cats into makeshift carriers—that and the bright orange sky in every direction is all I can remember from the blur. Heading out, I texted my supervisor, Elizabeth Hammack. We quickly composed a location list, hoping beyond hope that firemen could reach the park's most treasured archives.

Two days later, Susan heard from Elizabeth, who had devastating news: all of the park structures and offices were gone, including Susan's trailer and the well-stocked lending library she had been building for more than a decade. So, too, were the artifacts. Over the next several months, with housing for evacuees in very short supply, she, Dennis, MelMel, Princessa and the dogs went from living in a hotel to a cabin to a church to her brother's small trailer and finally, in April 2021, to Sunset State Beach in housing for State Parks employees.

When Susan and a group of docents returned to Big Basin at the end of 2020, they stood shoulder to shoulder in a memorial circle around one surviving structure at the Campfire Center—the fireplace—where so many delighted children had roasted apples.

None could put their experience that day into words, and no one tried. For Susan Blake, the greatest loss was her sense of identity—the place where she had worked, played and cherished every aspect of her life.

HEROIC RESPONSE TO AN INCONCEIVABLE CHALLENGE

In the very early morning hours of August 16, 2020, eleven thousand bolts of lightning ignited fires throughout California. At 6:41 a.m., what would soon be called the CZU Lightning Complex Fires began during a record-breaking heat wave. Initially uncontainable, it would take almost five weeks before Cal Fire announced the conflagration was contained. But not until a few days before Christmas was it officially extinguished. Of the 86,509 acres burned in Santa Cruz and San Mateo Counties, the 18,000 comprising Big Basin were 97 percent charred within three days. Yet on that third day, all five of the park's campgrounds were still fully occupied. Knowing that landscape from my earliest childhood, I felt something almost beyond miraculous had happened. Not a single person in Big Basin—whether staff or visitor—died or was injured, and all of the domestic pets whose owners had homes in the park survived.

Alex Tabone, an alumnus of the University of California at Santa Cruz, began his career with California State Parks first as an interpreter at the Santa Cruz Mission, followed by the last nine years as a ranger in the Santa Cruz Mountain sector. It's hard to imagine anyone better equipped for handling the challenge of wildfires in a park filled to capacity with campers. In addition to his role as the lead operations manager for Big Basin—knowing the terrain like the back of his hand—Alex has EMT certification and specialized training in fire management.

On August 16, already wide awake from the explosive lightning storm, Alex agreed to take the early shift and spent the day scouting for fires in and

In 2018, park concession employee Ryan Top delivered this fledgling marbled murrelet, found at Huckleberry campground, to Ranger Alex Tabone. Initially cared for by Native Animal Rescue, Alex released the bird, listed as endangered in California, at Waddell Beach. The California Department of Fish and Wildlife joined him for the successful send off. *Courtesy of Bill Rhoades Collection.*

around the Big Basin redwoods. The interagency teamwork with Cal Fire went well, and "together we had a pretty good handle on several small fires."

On Monday, continuing to coordinate the process of closures in areas adjacent to the park, he even began to feel encouraged about the future. The prescribed burn program—in place for decades—had been on hold for a few years due to uncooperative weather. Now, nature had taken over with a natural cycle of fire from the surge of lightning strikes. He envisioned how healthy small fires would be for the land, cleansing and rejuvenating areas impossible to reach with prescribed burns. Though in continuous phone contact with the incident command center, he saw only a small number of fire personnel due to so many other fires in the region.

For most of Tuesday, August 18, Alex worked near Highway One, the coastal section of Big Basin above Waddell Beach, serving as a resource advisor to a strike team for bulldozers constructing a fire line. But his feeling of progress quickly diminished mid-afternoon as fire whirls (small fire tornados) flared up from powerful winds. Alex made contact with his command staff, telling them to contact the fire incident command post: the fires were quickly growing. As soon as he walked down the hill off the fire line, he got a call from his boss, Scott Sipes, saying to head to Big Basin and begin evacuations. Alex vividly remembers Sipes telling him, jokingly, "You've been promoted." With the fire heading straight for the interior of the park, Alex had to get everyone out of all five campgrounds and Upper Sky Meadow and Lower

Sky Meadow immediately. (The Sky Meadow residence areas housed more than a dozen State Parks staff and their families in affordable houses, cabins and trailers inside the park.)

Driving from one side of the park to the other took at least forty minutes and every second counted. Once Alex and his team—Phil Bergman, Don Couthamel, Andrew Dobbs, Tyler Knapp, Patrick Rosso and James Weber—had made sure everyone was out of the 120-year-old Sempervirens Campground, they moved on to Huckleberry, well aware they had one thousand campers inside the park. To one couple's cavalier response to the evacuation order—"We will leave once we've had our dinner"—Alex said, "No, you will leave right now." Not until his trainee Don ordered them to "take only what you can't live without" did their blasé bubble burst, and out they ran.

The ranger group continued to make the rounds of the campgrounds, grateful that the COVID-19 pandemic had prevented any camping in backcountry areas, as those remote sites would have been nearly impossible to reach. With Alex on the PA system warning people to *get out now*, every few minutes, he switched and made contact with the command post, well aware that merged fires, traveling at record speed, had surrounded the park. What about his own house and that of his close friend and fellow ranger James Weber at Lower Sky Meadow?

> *It did cross my mind. But I swore an oath to protect people and to protect the park. Your oath is not just for days when everything is going well, but for when everything is going wrong. After several round trips to all five campgrounds, we felt confident we'd evacuated all the campers. Weber and Tyler Knapp took off to evacuate the residence areas. While doing the final notifications at Upper Sky Meadow, they located a spot fire burning near the houses and called for help.*
>
> *As soon as we arrived at Upper Sky Meadow, I yelled to Don to put on his yellows. Tyler was getting his gear ready and sized up the spot fire. At that point it was already one thousand square feet. I turned and looked up and there was a one-hundred-foot-high wall of fire. I yelled, "We've got to get out—it's time to go!"*

When their truck sped past Lower Sky Meadow, Alex took a brief glance toward the home he loved, in the best neighborhood he had ever known, hoping it was still there. His wife of three years, Collette, was out of harm's way in Santa Cruz with their cat Tamal and their twelve chickens. For the

Alex Tabone and his team (Bergman, Crouthamel, Dobbs, Knapp, Rosso and Weber) urgently evacuated more than one thousand campers on August 18, 2020. Although many had to abandon their campsites, everyone made it out safely. *Courtesy of Friends of Santa Cruz State Parks.*

friends who took them all in, Alex had recently constructed a chicken coup, which had yet to be occupied. Conveniently, it provided an immediate safe space for his and Collette's brood.

After four hours of sleep, Alex entered the command post for the morning briefing at 6:00 a.m. on August 19. "It felt eerie because of how few people attended. Things were going badly with everything having blown up overnight. We were told that "we only have enough resources for a five-thousand-acre fire and this is a sixty-thousand-acre fire." Those of us glued to the news in Santa Cruz heard the same devastating report: Cal Fire has only 10 percent of the resources needed to fight the CZU Lightning Complex fires raging throughout Santa Cruz and San Mateo Counties.

Alex, assigned to the State Parks structure salvage and damage assessment team, drove up Highway 236 just past the Boulder Creek Golf Course. What he saw seemed incomprehensible:

> *The landscape in every direction was totally cooked. We continued on with fires all around us and trees falling too fast to count. But there were no firefighters anywhere, maybe one or two engines that had been out all night on the way to get water and to refuel, but that was it. We used chainsaws to cut our way through the downed trees covering Highway 236.*
>
> *Once we got close enough to park headquarters, we could see that historic building was just totally gone. The famous auto tree next to it had sixty-foot-high flames coming out the top. Every building, all the history, completely gone. But I couldn't permit myself any emotions. As the EMT for our team, I had to stay focused on my responsibility to keep everyone safe from falling trees. Around mid-morning, just fifty feet away, we heard, then saw, a huge domino effect of one tree falling on another, crashing to the ground.*
>
> *Our team leader, Tim Hyland, said, "Let's circle up. When you accepted this assignment, you didn't know what you'd signed up for. Now you know. I can't guarantee your safety. What do you want to do?" We all—Alberto Bonilla, David Cowman, Don Crouthamel, Ryan Diller, Portia Halbert, Tim Hyland, Tim Reilly, Juan Villarino, Ashley Weil and I—were unanimous, determined to complete the remainder of our mission. We still needed to assess Upper Sky Meadow, the maintenance yard and Lower Sky Meadow.*
>
> *As we began the inspection of Lower Meadow, we were now on foot. When I rounded the corner turn in Sky Meadow Road, I looked ahead and saw there was nothing left. Falling to my knees, I had a sob. Our eight homes, our neighborhood, our community that gave me a sense of belonging, I would never see again. Tim held my shoulders. In the weeks ahead, I could cope only by throwing myself into the work of fighting the fires.*

Alex hasn't missed a day of work since the CZU Lightning Complex Fire began. But "Mr. Big Basin"—as he is known to many—has not been back to the park for some time. He's built a new chicken coup at New Brighton State Beach next to the house where California State Parks has relocated his family. He is currently assigned to a special enforcement team to prevent cannabis production in state parks—quite a change from his leadership role at Big Basin. For Alex Tabone, the greatest loss is the very deep connectedness—his everyday stewardship of our oldest state park—and the sense of community among state park employees who lived at Big Basin year-round.

A Dream Postponed

An innovative project at Big Basin launched in 2014 was very close to fruition in the summer of 2020. A memorandum of understanding between the Mountain Parks Foundation, California State Parks and Save the Redwoods League propelled a groundbreaking approach to visitor engagement. The idea, supported by an initial grant from Friends of Santa Cruz State Parks, emanated from Elizabeth Hammack, the state parks manager, who began her career at the park as a seasonal interpreter in the summer of 1986.

Attending Elizabeth's 2011 seminar—Interpretive Techniques for State Park Docents—I felt inspired by her modeling of how best to engage diverse audiences. When I first heard about the plan for Big Basin's new Nature Museum and Research Center in 2015, it sounded like something a very experienced interpreter like Elizabeth would have envisioned.

For Hammack, the most powerful method of engaging an audience—be it in person or in an exhibit—is "to make the subject matter so incredibly relevant to the individual that the subject is ultimately about the visitors themselves." She pictured a nature museum in which the visitor's experience is through the perspective of one of the animals that calls Big Basin home.

When entering the museum, you would first take a personality test to learn which animal you are, such as a deer, raccoon or perhaps a marbled murrelet. Moving through each exhibit, you discover what you eat, how you protect yourself and what you need to survive in your habitat. You learn how you interact with the other animals who may be the people joining you in the museum. Then afterward you visit the citizen science room to learn how your species is doing today through real-time studies that include ongoing research being conducted in Big Basin.

The Mountain Parks Foundation collaborated with Elizabeth and her staff to bring the immersion concept to life by raising $1.5 million in donations. Save the Redwoods League, in addition to its financial support, provided expertise and access to real-time scientific research to be showcased in the Citizen Science Room. Brenda Holmes, the foundation's executive director says, "We put our hearts into raising the money needed to make this dream a reality, enlisting partner organizations' help and engaging our community in a shared vision. Seeing the first pictures of the destruction left in the fire's wake was heartbreaking. It felt unreal—could our beautiful museum be destroyed?" What had so impressed me during a personal tour with Brenda in 2019 was how inviting and modern the new space would be while retaining relevant features from the past. (For before and after photos see color insert.)

Hammack and state parks staff member Jodi Apelt had worked together on the project since its inception. Hammack lamented, "All those years of research and planning that literally went up in smoke just months before we planned to open." Yet Hammack feels certain that when Big Basin is rebuilt, there will be a beautiful museum. Will it be exactly as planned? No. "The results of climate change will inform future decisions about where to build and how best to protect our old-growth forest. There will be new sustainable building practices and new technology, but we have our completed museum designs, and I think they will be incorporated to some degree in the new museum. Brenda Holmes and I hope the essence of the nature museum will be captured in some form. Imagining the new museum—with the stories that will be told both from the original designs and new perspectives—fills me with hope and even excitement about the possibilities for the future of the park."

"We who so love Big Basin are resilient, and together, we will create our next amazing chapter," says Holmes. (See Appendix B.)

Innovation in the Midst of Catastrophe

Jessica Kusz has an all-consuming passion for historic structures. Seeing the first batch of fire photos in August 2020, she knew she could use her position as the historic preservation project manager at Friends of Santa Cruz State Parks (Friends) to support the state parks staff in damage assessment. What exactly that would be quickly took shape, proving to be a bold and effective step in the park's path to recovery.

In Jessica's first conversation with State Archaeologist Mark Hylkema, they discussed the complete destruction and the need for an efficient reconnaissance project for precise documentation. But what existed for a thorough and quick assessment for close to 180 structural resources now lost? A program called Codifi—designed by archaeologists for archaeology, architectural history, forensics and conservation—immediately came to mind. Jessica had firsthand experience with the "paperless" process, having helped pilot it at the Castro Adobe State Historic Park in 2017 as part of an Archaeological Field Methods course for UC Santa Cruz undergraduates. The class—a creative collaboration—had multiple partners: UCSC, California State Parks, Albion Environmental Inc., Friends and BAC Northwest LLC.

What happened next showed how nimble a state bureaucracy can be when working with a proactive partner. Within a few weeks, state parks managers had signed off on the proposed plan, Friends raised $20,000 from the Community Foundation Santa Cruz County and the Codifi's owner committed to train the team. Using Codifi's app, they would record new data to archival standards with sub-meter accuracy, entirely offline!

On September 28, the reconnaissance/documentation team headed off in their caravan to Big Basin. Led by Denise Jaffke, the group consisted of eight other state parks staff members—Daren Andolina, Jennifer Daly, Stephanie Gallanosa, Mark Hylkema, Michael Jasinski, Kathleen Kennedy, Johanna Marty and Martin Rizzo-Martinez—together with Codifi owner Michael Ashley and Jessica Kusz. In compiling dozens of before and after photos, Jessica had prepared herself for the worst, but nothing could have prepared her for this:

> *Seeing the forest and the structures burned so completely—it was the first time in my life I had cried over losing historic buildings. The devastation felt so complete. Looking at where the administration building used to be, I could just feel the joyous memories, could hear the families getting trail guides and maps for their hikes through the redwoods, yet what contained*

On site at Big Basin. Senior State Archaeologist Denise Jaffke (*left*)—experienced with digital archaeology—confers with David Ashley of Codifi and Jessica Kusz of Friends. *Courtesy of Friends.*

them was all gone. There was something so final about the mounds of ashes and debris.

Turning to our task—where every piece of data would be digitized and electronically organized—some of us felt naked without our trusted clipboards and papers. But day by day, we'd come to appreciate the efficiency and precision of the new technology for taking photos, GPS locations and recording the building and archaeological remains. An added plus was that the program synchronized all the data every team member put in, nothing missed!

A determined group of partners with one new idea quickly pivoted to provide a credible solution to an otherwise mind-boggling challenge. The team's damage report—given to four federal and state agencies—met all the complex requirements, an essential step in developing a recovery plan. Jessica felt inspired by the "experience of proposing a dynamic and ecological approach to data collection and then being part of the team to first use it." The team's work has provided a model for post fire response across the state park system.

THE ARTIFACT THAT SURVIVED THE INFERNO

After so much loss, something magical happened. In my Saving Big Basin talks, I feature Carrie Stevens Walter along with other women and men. In the photos I use of her in PowerPoint presentations, she is clearly seen, but those were too small to meet my publisher's standards. I could not conceive of this book without a picture of Carrie that would do her justice. In a quandary, I turned to Charlene Duval for help because of her extensive skills as a historic resources consultant. After going through all the online databases of historic photographs and finding nothing, she tried a simple Google search and discovered an article written by Debbie Horton, the great-great-granddaughter of Carrie.[164] In the article, Debbie mentioned a portrait of Carrie that she saw hanging over her grandfather's desk throughout her childhood.

Charlene's expert sleuthing located Debbie, who told her that the family donated the painting to Big Basin long ago, where it resided in the director's office. But sadly, it had burned in the CZU fire. Even though Charlene and I were devastated at that news, I told her that the information didn't seem to make any sense. I'd never seen the painting at the park or heard it mentioned by any staff member, and there was no "director's office." I checked in with

Susan Blake, the longtime park interpreter, and she had no knowledge of the painting's existence and knew it hadn't been displayed. Okay, then where had it been residing all those years if Susan had not seen or heard of it? Who could possibly give us a lead now? Immediately, Charlene jumped back in:

I took a chance that state parks had it in their artifact cataloging system (TMS), maybe at least as a good photo. I asked our local state parks museum curator, Jennifer Daly, to check. More than a photo, she found the original! Someone had transferred the painting of Carrie from storage at Big Basin to Sacramento (the Statewide Museum Collections Center, California State Parks) in 2014! I contacted Debbie Horton; imagine her delight knowing the painting had survived.

Our next challenge was getting a photograph of the painting that met the publisher's standards. Jena Peterson, curator at the Collections Center, said that because of the pandemic, their photographer had been reassigned, and it could be a long wait. After discussing it with Traci, I asked if we could bring Gary Neier, our own photographer, explaining how essential Carrie Stevens Walter is to the accurate Big Basin story. I also told Jena that Mark Hylkema, Supervisor of the Cultural Resources Program, and Martin Rizzo-Martínez, Historian, for the Santa Cruz State Parks District had written the book's foreward. Since Mark's reputation is known throughout the system, maybe name-dropping would help.

Soon after, I heard from Jena, who had consulted her supervisor. She found another state parks staff person, an excellent art photographer, who took a perfect photo in just the right light for an oil painting. Despite reduced hours, Jena quickly worked out the paperwork and use fee with Traci. With receipt of the payment, she uploaded the digital photo of Carrie's portrait to us.

Laying eyes on the painting felt incredible! I realized A.P. Hill probably painted it for the Walter family after Carrie's death in 1907. To me, it was as if she had emerged from the ashes of Big Basin, claiming her indispensable role on the team that created our beloved State Park.

As I looked at Carrie's museum-worthy portrait, I felt profound reassurance. My aunt Jennie asked me to promise I would never forget how the Santa Cruz redwoods were saved. With the uncanny survival of this one artifact in perfect condition, I'm confident the true story will not be erased again. (See the color insert for the long-lost portrait of Carrie Stevens Walter.)

AFTERWORD

My optimism for Big Basin's future derives from what these many individuals, beginning with the earliest inhabitants, have taught me about resilient commitment. As I continue to ponder what a fresh and flourishing approach to park stewardship might look like in the twenty-first century, here is one example based on my deep roots in Santa Cruz.

On my father's side (Bliss), I am fourth-generation Santa Cruzan, and on my mother's side (Imus), I am seventh. The Imuses, who helped build Santa Cruz, would never have made it across the Sierra had it not been for the humanity of the Paiute tribe. Chief Truckee rescued the stranded Imus party and guided them safely to Sutter's Fort in 1846. Most significantly, the wagon train of pioneers trusted their well-being entirely to the Paiutes.[165] We, as Santa Cruzans and as a State Parks system, now have an open door to embrace a similar kind of trust.

Acknowledging that the acquisition of Big Basin—before it became public—has been linked to the mixed-ancestry "Dakota Sioux scrip," preceded by the longstanding ancestral stewardship of the Cotoni people, provides an opportunity for even deeper recognition. This is especially critical because in addition to a diversity of local Indigenous community members who recognize the Cotoni as their ancestral relatives, California is home to the largest and most diverse Native American population in the country. How crucial it is that we make a wholehearted commitment to enduring collaboration that blends both indigenous values and, most importantly, a prominent and continued Indigenous presence within all of our public programs at Big Basin State Park.

ACKNOWLEDGEMENTS

An environmental historian at Rutgers University, Susan Schrepfer played an indispensable role in the early years of this journey. In addition to her expert advice, she imbued me with the historical significance of my research into women's voices as essential to saving Big Basin. I am also pleased to acknowledge Annette Boushey Holland, my Stanford classmate, whose keen insights and talent helped my thinking about this presentation of redwood preservation history.

I am deeply indebted to Colin Scully, whose faith in the power of the story and exceptional mentoring kept me moving forward, especially during the rough patches. Gary Krisel's frank and perceptive feedback in 2018 pushed the narrative well beyond what I had ever envisioned.

In 2019, Patrick Shea, former director of the Bureau of Land Management, brought his class from Stanford on my historic walking tour of the Santa Cruz Mountain Redwoods. Enrolled in Public Land: A History, sponsored by the Bill Lane Center of the American West, the students' insightful questions propelled my thorough investigation into the original owner of Big Basin. For that, I needed the help of someone with firsthand knowledge of relevant Minnesota terrain. Writer Sally Iverson was an ideal collaborator for chapter 1. A native Minnesotan, her up-close familiarity with important locations and years of experience as a staff member at the University of Minnesota Libraries, were a perfect fit.

Heartfelt thanks to the many individuals who helped us untangle the complexities of the Sioux scrip and its deliberate misuse to acquire Big

Basin: Gary Clayton Anderson, University of Oklahoma; Chris Belland, Barbara Bezat and Heidi Heller, Minnesota Historical Society; Halley Hair, South Dakota State Historical Society; Jeffery Hartley, National Archives and Records Administration; Frederick L. Johnson, author; Carla Joinson, author; Rick Lybeck, Minnesota State University, Mankato; Katherine Nelsen, University of Minnesota Libraries; David Ress, journalist/author; and Don Schwartz, Lake City Historical Society, Minnesota.

Foundational to my study of the Santa Cruz Mountain redwoods is *Coast Redwood: A Natural and Cultural History*, with a significant portion by Sandy Lydon. Thank you to several other Santa Cruz–based historians who made their robust photo and archive collections available and helped solve challenging research questions: Ross Eric Gibson, Rick Hyman, Deborah Osterberg, Frank Perry and Lisa Robinson. Also, much appreciation to photographers Shmuel Thaller and SLV Steve, along with tree feller Bruce Baker, for their contributions to the color insert. Ronnie Trubeck's generosity with both her collection and extensive San Lorenzo Valley contacts made it possible to fill gaps in the visual story. As a consultant, Randall Brown provided extensive newspaper research and transcriptions about key individuals and events as well as his insights. Barrie Rose Bliss, Randall Brown, Charlene Duval, Elizabeth Humphrey, Sally Iverson and Martin Rizzo-Martinez contributed valuable reviews for sections of the manuscript. The afterword reflects very thoughtful feedback from Stan Rushworth, Martin Rizzo-Martinez and Mark Hylkema. A big thanks to Bonny Hawley for her rigorous feedback on the next-to-last draft and subsequent proofreading. Samuel Bliss contributed much to the content editing, and copy editor Marty Mee Dunn went well beyond expectations with her exceptional eye for clarity, consistency and flow.

Nearing the publisher's deadline, many of the endnotes were no longer available. Ruth Cusick of the Santa Cruz Historic Newspaper Indexing Project stepped in and worked nonstop for a month to recapture them. Barrie Rose Bliss contributed her expert ability to organize and format all of the endnotes and bibliography. Wyatt Young created the index. Their focused efforts gave me the time to craft a whole new ending.

A cataclysmic fire consumed the park overnight in August 2020. As word spread about my almost-finished book, I felt the outpouring of love for Big Basin as local photographers, historians, hikers and individuals I had never met offered any help they could provide. But with no expertise in urban wildfires, what could I possibly write for an epilogue? Listening to many experts, I realized that insider voices were missing from the story: the experiences of those frontline individuals whose lives had been shattered but whose commitment continues. Susan Blake, Elizabeth Hammack, Brenda Holmes and Alex Tabone generously gave of their time for interviews and carefully reviewed and approved my writing of their stories. Thanks to each of them, together with Jessica Kusz, for an epilogue that makes a unique contribution to a reimagined park for future generations.

For the book's visual content, I've had a remarkable team. Nature photographer Bill Rhoades, with fourteen years of experience as a Big Basin trail guide, contributed many of the photos in the color insert. The corresponding captions reflect his extensive knowledge of the park's natural and cultural history. For the black-and-white photos, Charlene Duval, historian at the Sourisseau Academy at San Jose State University, left not a single stone unturned to help find the best-fit photographs, many never before published. Additionally, she located key descendants Debbie Horton (great-great-granddaughter of Carrie Stevens Walter) and Colleen Cassin (great-granddaughter of Louise Coffin Jones), whose contributions and images have enriched our understanding of two women who gave so much to the cause. In composing captions for many of the black-and-white images, I received historical "gems" from Ross Gibson, expert knowledge of the park from Bill Rhoades and tireless fact checking from Charlene Duval of the Sourisseau Academy.

Managing all aspects of the photos from twenty institutional archives, each with a different set of procedures, together with those from several private collectors, was a Herculean task. Gary Neier, who began his career with the National Forest Service, accomplished it with humor and dedication.

Due to the COVID-19 pandemic, all archives were indefinitely closed to the public. Staff were only available for limited hours at most institutions. Nonetheless, they went out of their way to help Gary, Charlene and me to locate and acquire the most appropriate representations in their collections. Our gratitude to Kelci Baughman McDowell, Santa Clara University Special Collections; April Halberstadt, San Jose Woman's Club; Nancy Jenner, California State Parks; Eben Lehman, Forest History Society; Leilani Marshall, Sourisseau Academy; Lauren Menzies, the Society of California Pioneers; Becky Miller, Natural Resources & Public Health Library at the University of California, Berkeley; Cate Mills, History San Jose; Timothy Nolan, Stanford University Library Special Collections; Jena Peterson, California State Parks; Lisa Robinson, San Lorenzo Valley Historical Society and Museum; Natalie Snoyman, Mill Valley Public Library; Jeff Thomas, San Francisco Public Library; Victor Willis, Santa Cruz Public Library;

Wyatt Young, Santa Cruz Museum of Art & History; Special Collections, University of California at Santa Cruz; Bancroft Library, University of California, Berkeley; and Friends of Santa Cruz State Parks.

I am grateful to those who gave in unique ways to help bring this work to fruition: Hal Anjo, Holly Alexander, Jone Balesteri, the Bibbey family, Jeff Canepa, Jeff Bosshard, Eddy Budworth, Jeff Canepa, Tod Gregory, Margaret Fitzsimmons, Lynn Hill, Matt Karl, Sue Kerr, Dylan McManus, Ryan Masters, Joe Michalak, Marion Pokriots, Liz Pollack, Laura Schultz, Pat Shea, Judy Steen, Casey Tefertiller, David Tirri, Daniel Williford, Shelly Woolf and Mary Wood. Lorri Ditz McCarthy, my classmate from high school and college, gave her patient, listening ear for a decade. Among her treasured childhood memories are the Ditz family vacations at Sempervirens Camp.

I could not have hoped for a more supportive and creative editor than Laurie Krill of The History Press.

ORIGINAL OWNERS OF THE SIOUX SCRIP USED TO PURCHASE BIG BASIN ACRES

Scrip Owner	Acres
Charles Augi	320
Joseph Demarias	80
Augustin Freynur	80
Margaret Carrier	580
Joseph Decontean	40
David Gummiel	160
Joseph Bird	80
Mary H. Dupuis	160
Joseph Doncetle	200
Lydia Ann Brown	160
Lucy Frazier	160

Source: "A Land Grab," *San Francisco Examiner*, September 24, 1883.

BIG BASIN NATURE MUSEUM & RESEARCH CENTER

Donor Recognition Plaque
Main Exhibit Room

Mountain Parks Foundation
Save the Redwoods League
Evelyn Tilden Mohrhardt Fund
Anonymous
California Cultural and Historical Endowment
Joseph and Vera Long Foundation
Monterey Peninsula Foundation
Dean Witter Foundation
Thomas O. Brown Foundation
Joe Griffin and Linda Fawcett
Melvin and Geraldine Hoven Foundation
The Lavenstein Family
Friends of Santa Cruz State Parks
Sempervirens Fund
California State Parks Foundation
Clif Bar Foundation
Carol Fuller
Ralph Britton
Lisa and Tim Robinson
Traci Bliss

Source: Major Donors, Mountain Parks Foundation 2020

NOTES

Foreword

1. Rizzo-Martinez, *We Are Not Animals*.
2. For details about the most well-known Indigenous survivor of the California Missions, see Bliss and Brown, *Evergreen Cemetery of Santa Cruz*, 15, 41, 63–64, and Rizzo-Martinez, *We Are Not Animals*.

Chapter 1

3. A detailed history and useful map are provided by Brohough, *Sioux and Chippewa Half-Breed Scrip*.
4. Brohough, *Sioux and Chippewa Half-Breed Scrip*, 23–42. For a detailed account of both treaties and the exact pieces of scrip for determining acreage for the "half-breeds."
5. Ress's book, especially chapter 6, together with his answers to several questions, were essential for helping sort out the intricate complexities of the topic. Ress, *Half-Breed Tracts*; Frederick L. Johnson, "'Half-Breed' Tract."
6. *San Francisco Examiner*, September 24, 1883, 1:3.
7. Bender, "Valuable People," 17–18.
8. Folwell, *History of Minnesota*, 485.
9. Ibid., 484.

10. Various terms are used to describe "half-breeds." My decision to use mixed-ancestry Dakota is based on the work of Jimmy Sweet. Sweet, "Native Suffrage," 108.
11. Anderson offers a vivid description of the camp, including the departures of those incarcerated. Andersen, *Massacre in Minnesota*, 273.
12. Millikan, "Great Treasure," 14.
13. Anderson details the confusion over how many Indians died at Fort Snelling and when. It is not known during what months the scrip was obtained from the "half-breeds." Andersen, *Massacre in Minnesota*, 330.
14. Ress, *Half Breed Tracts*, 86.
15. The details of Chapman's life are found in Robert Long's well-documented dissertation. Sioux Scrip is not part of the focus. Long, "Fresno County, California," 45.
16. *Santa Cruz Surf*, September 14, 1883.
17. Long, "Fresno County," 45.
18. Ibid., 114.

Chapter 2

19. For a specific description of how the Southern Pacific wielded power, see Christensen and Gerston, "Rise of the McClatchy's," 11.
20. Ralph Smith, S*anta Cruz Surf*, May 22, 1897, 2.
21. Senator Leland Stanford, January 10, 1862, governors.library.ca.gov.
22. *Record-Union*, November 8, 1887, 2:3.
23. *Santa Cruz Surf*, August 29, 1889, 3:5.
24. In addition to illuminating the conflict between Huntington and Stanford, Tutorow provides a few examples of the close relationship between the young Hopkins and Stanford. Tutorow, *Leland Stanford*, 264.
25. *Santa Cruz Surf*, August 1, 1891, 7:4.
26. Ibid., March 26, 1892, 2:6.
27. Schrepfer, *Fight to Save the Redwoods*, 10.
28. I developed a deep appreciation for the depth of Professor Dudley's Big Basin expert knowledge thanks to his papers and field notes available at Stanford University Special Collections. William Russel Dudley Papers (SC0558). Department of Special Collections and University Archives, Stanford University Libraries, Stanford, Calif. Box 2: folder 20, 27; box 3: folder 14, 15, 18; box 4: folder 8; box 5: folder 11; box 17: folder 4.
29. William Dudley, *San Jose Evening News*, June 7, 1902, 1:1.

30. In the early 1800s, Jennie's grandfather Abel Bliss was committed to the antislavery movement in Massachusetts. He held a leadership role in the state. Merrick and Foster, eds, *History of Wilbraham*, 255.

31. *Santa Cruz Sentinel*, May 27, 1884, 3; May 29, 1884.

32. *San Francisco Bulletin*, July 11, 1891.

33. At the conclusion of the Big Basin campaign, Taylor described the importance of Clarke's early photographs when he alone was documenting Big Basin for the public. *Santa Cruz Surf*, March 23, 1901.

34. *Santa Cruz Sentinel*, October 26, 1892, 3:2; *Santa Cruz Surf*, October 26, 1892, 5:3.

35. *Santa Cruz Surf*, December 4, 1893, 3:1.

36. Eldredge, "Banking in California," 456–7.

37. *Record-Union*, April 16, 1894, 1:3.

38. For more about the rebuilt bank after the 1894 fire see Brown and Bliss, *Santa Cruz's Seabright*, 28.

39. "Hot Stuff," *Santa Cruz Surf*, September 13, 1894, 4:4.

40. For a detailed account see Bliss and Brown, *Evergreen Cemetery of Santa Cruz*, 71–72.

41. *Santa Cruz Surf*, July 17, 1897, 3:4.

42. A.A. Taylor's editorial lauded Jeter's role as president of the Senate: "He won the respect, admiration, and confidence of every member on the floor, and retired with a degree of goodwill rarely enjoyed." *Santa Cruz Surf*, January 12, 1899, 2.

43. Catherine Brown Smith, "Sex Lines in Literature," *San Francisco Call*, July 12, 1895, 3:3.

44. Rice, *Women of Our Valley*, 32.

45. Jones, *Travel Journals*.

46. Unger, *Beyond Nature's Housekeepers: American Women in Environmental History*, 91. Also, this perspective was clearly conveyed by Susan Schrepfer in conversations during the summer of 2013.

47. An extensive account of these events is found in Osterberg, *Historic Tales of Henry Cowell Redwoods*, 120–2.

48. For tourism at Big Trees Grove, see Osterberg, *Historic Tales of Henry Cowell Redwoods*, especially chapter 8.

49. *San Jose Mercury*, reprinted in *Santa Cruz Sentinel*, April 29, 1900, 4:1.

50. *Santa Cruz Evening Sentinel*, March 7, 1900, 3:3.

Chapter 3

51. Nickliss provides a thorough and compelling account of Phoebe Heart's life and legacy. Nickliss, *Phoebe Apperson Hearst*.
52. *San Francisco Examiner*, February 11, 1900, 23:1.
53. *San Francisco Call*, February 24, 1900, 6:4.
54. For the full story of the prolonged Calaveras campaigns see Engbeck, *Enduring Giants*, 95–110.
55. *Santa Cruz Surf*, March 17, 1900, 2:2.
56. *Santa Cruz Sentinel*, August 4, 1898, 1:1.
57. Brown, *San Lorenzo Valley Water District* provides a detailed view of both Middleton and Hopkins and how they influenced the history of the San Lorenzo Valley.
58. *Santa Cruz Surf*, April 23, 1900, 4:5.
59. Bliss and Brown, "Saving Big Basin Heroes and Heroines," 117–28. This early article provided a nascent understanding of the team effort that created Big Basin.
60. *Santa Cruz Sentinel*, originally from *San Jose Mercury*, May 3, 1900, 1:5.
61. *Santa Cruz Surf*, May 17, 1900, 4:2.

Chapter 4

62. *San Francisco Chronicle*, May 27, 1900, 32.
63. Ibid. For the importance of forests for nineteenth-century Methodism, for example, "The groves were God's first temples," see Richey, *Methodism in the American Forest*, 167.
64. *Santa Cruz Sentinel*, June 13, 1900, 4:2–3.
65. Carrie Stevens Walter, *San Francisco Chronicle*, May 27, 1900, 32.
66. *San Francisco Chronicle*, May 27, 1900, 32; *Santa Cruz Surf*, May 13, 1901, 7:2.
67. *Overland Monthly*, August 1900, 135–9.
68. *San Francisco Chronicle*, November 10, 1900, 10:3.
69. *Mountain Echo*, November 24, 1900, 2:11.
70. *Santa Cruz Sentinel*, November 22, 1900, 1:1–2.
71. Ibid., November 25, 1900, 2:1.
72. *Santa Cruz Surf*, September 14, 1901, 2:1.
73. Nikiliss provides detailed accounts of Phoebe Hearst's relationship to women's suffrage.
74. *San Francisco Call*, December 22, 1900, 5:7.

Chapter 5

75. *Santa Cruz Surf*, January 28, 1901, 1:3–4.
76. *San Francisco Call*, March 5, 1901, 7:5.
77. *Sacramento Bee*, March 5, 1901, 5:3–4.
78. *Santa Cruz Sentinel*, March 16, 1901, 1:7.
79. Ibid., June 3, 1915, 6:4–5.
80. Ibid., April 13, 1901, 1:1.
81. Martin, *History of Santa Cruz County*, 86.
82. Laura Lovel White, *Santa Cruz Sentinel*, June 3, 1915, 6:4–5.

Chapter 6

83. *San Jose Evening News*, August 5, 1901, 5:2–3.
84. *San Francisco Call*, August 11, 1901, 21:3; August 14, 1901, 13:3–4.
85. *San Jose Evening News*, November 7, 1902, 4:4–5.
86. *Evening Sentinel*, August 13, 1902, 1:3–4.
87. Jones, "First Impressions," 29.
88. *Sacramento Bee*, January 23, 1902, 2:2–3.
89. *Santa Cruz Sentinel*, January 25, 1902, 3:4.
90. Ibid.
91. *San Francisco Call*, January 24, 1902, 1:1–3, 2:5.
92. *Santa Cruz Sentinel*, January 24, 1902, 1:3.
93. Christensen and Gerston, "Rise of the McClatchys," 8:2
94. For a compelling analysis comparing and contrasting California's early newspaper dynasties see Christensen and Gerston, "Rise of the McClatchys," 8–15.
95. *Santa Cruz Surf*, July 17, 1902, 6:2; August 1, 1902, 4:1; *Sacramento Bee*, July 30, 1902, 4:2–4.
96. *Santa Cruz Sentinel*, September 12, 1902, 3:4.
97. *San Francisco Examiner*, September 25, 1902, 5:5.
98. *Santa Cruz Evening News*, August 16, 1910, 1:6-7.
99. *San Francisco Chronicle*, September 26, 1902, 6:2.
100. *Sacramento Bee*, September 27, 1902, 14:5; *Sacramento Bee*, September 27, 1902, 16:1–7.
101. Piwarzyk and Miller, *Valley of Redwoods*, 30.
102. Gibson, "History of De Laveaga," 23–24.

Chapter 7

103. This volume is the compilation of dozens of poems by Walter. Walter, "In Memory of Mrs. E.O. Smith," in *Rose-Ashes and Other Poems*, 102.
104. *Evening Sentinel*, September 10, 1904, 1:1–2; September 9, 1904, 1:3–4.
105. *San Jose Evening News*, September 10, 1904, 5:1–2.
106. Taylor, "Save the Redwoods," in *California Redwood Park*, 24.
107. Pardee, "Conservation in California," 381.
108. Taylor, "Timber Cutting," in *California Redwood Park*, 52.
109. Taylor, "The Big Fire," in *California Redwood Park*, 51.
110. "Enrico Caruso and the 1906 Earthquake," in *The Sketch*, reprinted in *The Theatre* 6, no. 65 (July 1906), http://www.sfmuseum.net/1906/ew19.html.
111. Fradkin, *Great Earthquake*, 45.
112. "Enrico Caruso."
113. This account focuses on the economic consequences. Eldredge, "San Francisco," 505–21.
114. Hull concludes her photo essay with this summary: "A century removed from the calamities in San Francisco we are forced to consider not just ecological consequences of natural disasters and our response to them, but our own role in compounding such disasters." Hull, "Redwood in the 1906 San Francisco Earthquake," 35.
115. Everett, "Lumber Men," 341.
116. *Berkeley Gazette*, May 25, 1906, 9:3; *Santa Cruz Sentinel*, July 27, 1906, 9; Everett, "Lumber Men," 341. For the effects of the earthquake on the San Lorenza Valley see Hammond, *California Central Coast*, 140.
117. *Evening Sentinel*, July 27, 1906, 7:3.
118. *Santa Cruz Weekly Sentinel*, May 4, 1907, 5:2.

Chapter 8

119. *Evening Sentinel*, May 23, 1907, 5:2–3; *Santa Cruz Sentinel*, June 9, 1907, 9:2.
120. *Santa Cruz Sentinel*, February 21, 1908, 2:4.
121. Taylor, "Timber Cutting," in *California Redwood Park*, 53.
122. *Santa Cruz Sentinel*, March 13, 1908, 1:2.
123. *Sacramento Bee*, March 19, 1908, 9:2; *Santa Cruz Sentinel*, March 17, 1908, 3:1–2.

NOTES TO PAGES 110–123

124. *San Francisco Chronicle*, March 15, 1908, 20:1; *Santa Cruz Sentinel*, March 25, 1908, 3:2; *Evening News Mountain Echo*, March 24, 1908, 1:5–6.

125. *San Francisco Call*, March 24, 1908, 4:7; March 25, 1908, 6:2.

126. Pardee, "Conservation in California," 394. For a contemporary discussion of conservation versus preservation see Andrews, "Conservation or Preservation."

Chapter 9

127. Bliss and Brown, "Saratoga Road to Big Basin," 135–7; *Santa Cruz Sentinel*, January 7, 1913, 4:3.

128. De Vries, *Grand and Ancient Forest*, 56.

129. For a detailed account of the event see Osterberg, *Historic Tales of Henry Cowell Redwoods*, 134–6.

130. *Santa Cruz Sentinel*, March 12, 1910, 8:5.

131. *Santa Cruz Evening News*, April 26, 1910, 1:3–4.

132. *Mercury News*, August 28, 1910, 5:2–4, 8:2–7.

133. Ibid.

134. *Santa Cruz Sentinel*, January 7, 1911, 1:1; January 24, 1911, 1:5; February 1, 1911, 5:4.

135. Ibid., February 11, 1911, 8:4–5.

136. Ibid., February 17, 1911, 3:3.

137. *Santa Cruz Evening News*, March 3, 1911, 1:6; March 10, 1911, 1:7.

138. Jordan, *Days of a Man*, 518.

139. Lydon, *Coast Redwood*, 128–30.

140. *Sacramento Bee*, May 27, 1912, 1:6–7.

141. Nolan, "Half Breed," 1–2.

Chapter 10

142. *Santa Cruz Evening News*, January 27, 1921, 1:7; January 31, 1921, 2:2–3.

143. In September 1886, Jeter received encouragement about the prospects for the Grove someday becoming a public park when he took Frederick Law Olmsted and Frederick Jr. on a tour of the area. *Santa Cruz Evening News*, July 18, 1928, 3:2–4.

144. *Santa Cruz Evening News*, June 13, 1922, 5:2–3.

145. Ibid., August 12, 1925, 6:1–6.

146. For more on Taylor's contributions to Santa Cruz see Bliss and Brown, *Evergreen Cemetery of Santa Cruz*, 62, 80, 82 and 83.

147. For the follow-up action by the chamber see *Santa Cruz Evening News*, December 28, 1925, 1:3.

148. *Santa Cruz Evening News*, January 18, 1926, 5:1.

149. Ibid., April 15, 1926, 3:1.

150. Ibid., March 9, 1928, 1:2–3.

151. Ibid.

152. See Appendix B in Osterberg's *Historic Tales of Henry Cowell Redwoods State Park* for my summaries (with Randall Brown) of eleven movies made at the Grove.

153. Once married, Jennie became very private and avoided publicity. Gaps in the family history passed down from my grandfather were mostly filled during interviews. See interviewees at the end of the bibliography.

154. *Santa Cruz Evening News*, July 3, 1929, 9:8.

155. Ibid., September 20, 1929, 1:2–3.

156. Okrent, *Guarded Gate*, 205; Schrepfer, *Fight to Save the Redwoods*, 43–45; Farmer, *Trees in Paradise*, 68–72. A heartfelt and essential piece is provided by Hodder, "Reckoning with League Founders'."

157. Frank, *Local Girl Makes History*, 20.

158. *Santa Cruz Evening News*, May 12, 1934, 1:2, 2:2–3. For moving tributes to Jeter's Character see *Santa Cruz Evening News*, May 8,1934, 9:1.

159. Osterberg, *Historic Tales of Henry Cowell Redwoods*, 151.

160. Frank A. Perry, *Lime Kiln Legacies*, 81.

161. *Santa Cruz Sentinel*, February 2, 1955, 1:5–6.

Epilogue

162. Stienstra says in his description of Big Basin, "No matter what your age, a trip to Big Basin redwoods…can feel as if you're pushing the restart button on life." Stienstra, *Outdoors*, 72.

163. Bliss and Brown, "Saving Big Basin Heroes and Heroines."

164. Horton, "About the Author," 7–8.

Afterword

165. For specifics about Chief Truckee see Bliss and Brown, *Evergreen Cemetery of Santa Cruz*, 20, 26, 41.

BIBLIOGRAPHY

Books

Andersen, Gary Clayton. *Massacre in Minnesota: The Dakota War of 1862, the Most Violent Ethnic Conflict in American History*. Norman: University of Oklahoma Press, 2019.

Barbour, Michael G., et al. *Coast Redwood: A Natural and Cultural History*. Edited by John Evarts and Marjorie Popper. Los Olivos, CA: Cachuma Press, 2001.

Bliss, Traci, and Randall Brown. *Evergreen Cemetery of Santa Cruz*. Charleston SC: The History Press, 2020.

Brohough, Gustav O. *Sioux and Chippewa Half-Breed Scrip and Its Application to the Minnesota Pine Lands*. India: Pranava Books, 1906.

Brown, Randall C. *The San Lorenzo Valley Water District: A History*. Boulder Creek, CA: San Lorenzo Valley Water District, 2011.

Brown, Randall, and Traci Bliss. *Santa Cruz's Seabright*. Charleston, SC: Arcadia Publishing, 2017.

Christofferson, Bill. *The Man from Clear Lake: Earth Day Founder Senator Gaylord Nelson*. Madison: University of Wisconsin Press, 2009.

Clark, Donald T. *Santa Cruz County Place Names*. Scotts Valley, CA: Krestrel Press, 2008.

Clayton, John. *Natural Rivals*. New York: Pegasus, 2019.

Crespí, Juan. *A Description of Distant Roads: Original Journals of the First Expedition into California, 1769–1770*. Edited by Alan K. Brown. San Diego, CA: San Diego State University Press, 2001.

Department of Parks and Recreation. *Big Basin State Park: Final General Plan and Environmental Impact Report*. Sacramento: California Department of Parks and Recreation, 2013.

De Vries, Carolyn. *Grand and Ancient Forest: The Story of Andrew P. Hill and Big Basin Redwoods State Park*. Fresno, CA: Valley Press, 1978.

Egan, Timothy. *The Big Burn: Teddy Roosevelt and the Fire That Saved America*. Boston: Houghton Mifflin Harcourt, 2009.

Elliott, Russell R., and William D. Rowley. *History of Nevada*. Lincoln: University of Nebraska Press, 1987.

Engbeck, Joseph H. *The Enduring Giants: The Giant Sequoias*. Sacramento: California Department of Parks and Recreation, 1988.

Engbeck, Joseph H., and Philip Hyde. *State Parks of California, from 1864 to the Present*. Portland, OR: Graphic Arts Publishing Company, 1980.

Farmer, Jared. *Trees in Paradise: A California History*. New York: W.W. Norton, 2013.

Folsom, Burton W. *The Myth of the Robber Barons: A New Look at the Rise of Big Business in America*. Herndon, VA: Young America's Foundation, 1991.

Folwell, William Watts. *A History of Minnesota*. Vol. 1. St. Paul: Minnesota Historical Society, 1922.

Fradkin, Philip L. *The Great Earthquake and Firestorms of 1906: How San Francisco Nearly Destroyed Itself*. Berkeley: University of California Press, 2005.

Frank, Dana. *Local Girl Makes History: Exploring Northern California's Kitsch Monuments*. San Francisco, CA: City Lights Foundation, 2007.

Hamman, Rick. *California Central Coast Railway*. Boulder, CO: Pruett Publishing Company, 1980.

Hempton, David. *Methodism: Empire of the Spirit*. New Haven, CT: Yale University Press, 2005.

Johnson, Ayana Elizabeth, and Katherine K. Wilkinson, eds. *All We Can Save: Truth, Courage, and Solutions for the Climate Crisis*. New York: Random House, 2020.

Jordan, David Starr. *The Days of a Man: Being Memories of a Naturalist, Teacher and Minor Prophet of Democracy Vol. 1, 1851–1899*. New York, Yonkers-on-Hudson, World Book Company, 1922.

Keator, Glenn, Linda Yamane and Anne Lewis. *In Full View: Three Ways of Seeing California Plants*. Berkeley, CA: Heyday Books, 1995.

Margolin, Malcolm. *The Ohlone Way: Indian Life in the San Francisco–Monterey Bay Area*. Berkeley, CA: Heyday Books, 1978.

Martin, Edward L. *History of Santa Cruz County*. Los Angeles: Historic Record Company, 1911.

Martin, Justin. *Genius of Place: The Life of Frederick Law Olmstead*. Boston: Da Capo Press, 2011.

Merrick, Charles L., and Phillip B. Foster, eds. *History of Wilbraham U.S.A: Bicentennial Edition, 1763–1963*. Bennington, VT: Polygraphic Company of America, 1964.

Miller, Michael L., and Robert W. Piwarzyk. *Valley of Redwoods: A Guide to Henry Cowell Redwoods State Park*. Felton, CA: Mountain Parks Foundation, 2006.

Momaday, N. Scott. *Earth Keeper: Reflections on the American Land*. New York: HarperCollins, 2020.

Nickliss, Alexandra M. *Phoebe Apperson Hearst: A Life of Power and Politics*. Lincoln: University of Nebraska Press, 2018.

Okrent, Daniel. *The Guarded Gate: Bigotry, Eugenics, and the Law That Kept Two Generations of Jews, Italians, and Other European Immigrants out of America*. New York: Scribner, 2020.

Osterberg, Deborah. *Historic Tales of Henry Cowell Redwoods State Park: Big Trees Grove*. Charleston, SC: The History Press, 2020.

Payne, Stephen. *A Howling Wilderness: The Summit Road of the Santa Cruz Mountains*. Los Gatos, CA: Loma Prieta Publishing, 1978.

Perry, Frank A. *Lime Kiln Legacies: The History of the Lime Industry in Santa Cruz County*. Santa Cruz, CA: Santa Cruz Museum of Art & History, 2007.

Powers, Richard. *The Overstory*. New York: W.W. Norton, 2018.

Preston, Richard. *The Wild Trees*. New York: Random House, 2008.

Pyne, Stephen J. *America's Fires: A Historical Context for Policy and Practice*. Durham, NC: Forest History Society, 2009.

Ress, David. "Scrip and the Taking of the Minnesota Half Breed Tract." In *The Half Breed Tracts in Early National America: Changing Concepts of Land and Place*. London: Palgrave Pivot, 2019.

Rice, Bertha M. *The Women of Our Valley*. Vol. 1. N.p.: 1955.

Richey, Russell E. *Methodism in the American Forest*. New York: Oxford University Press, 2015.

Rizzo-Martinez, Martin. *We Are Not Animals: Indigenous Politics of Survival, Rebellion, and Reconstitution in 19th Century California*. Lincoln: University of Nebraska Press, 2021.

Robinson, Lisa, ed. *Redwood Logging and Conservation in the Santa Cruz Mountains: A Split History*. Santa Cruz, CA: Santa Cruz Museum of Art & History at the McPherson Center, 2014.

Rushworth, Stan. *Diaspora's Children*. Topanga, CA: Hand and Hand Publishing, 2020.

Rutkow, Eric. *American Canopy: Trees, Forests, and the Making of a Nation*. New York: Scribner, 2013.

Schrepfer, Susan R. *The Fight to Save the Redwoods: A History of the Environmental Reform, 1917–1978*. Madison: University of Wisconsin Press, 1983.

———. *Nature's Altars: Mountains, Gender, and American Environmentalism*. Lawrence: University Press of Kansas, 2005.

Spiro, Jonathan Peter. *Defending the Master Race: Conservation, Eugenics, and the Legacy of Madison Grant*. Lebanon, NH: University Press of New England, 2009.

Stanger, Frank. *Sawmills in the Redwoods*. San Mateo, CA: San Mateo County Historical Society, 1967.

Stevens, Stanley D. *Names on the Map: History of the 1889 "Hatch Map," the "First" Official Map of Santa Cruz County, California*. Santa Cruz, CA: Santa Cruz Museum of Art & History, 2020.

Stienstra, Tom. *Outdoors: A Guide to the Bay Area's Best State and Regional Parks, Recreation and Wilderness Areas*. San Francisco: *San Francisco Chronicle*, 2019.

Taylor, Arthur A. *California Redwood Park*. Sacramento, CA: W. Richardson, 1912.

Tutorow, Norman E. *Leland Stanford: Man of Many Careers*. Menlo Park, CA: Pacific Coast Publishers, 1971.

Unger, Nancy C. *Beyond Nature's Housekeepers: American Women in Environmental History*. New York: Oxford University Press, 2012.

Walter, Carrie Stevens. *Rose-Ashes and Other Poems*. Watsonville, CA: Watsonville Press, 2002.

Waziyatawin, PhD (Wilson, Angela Cavender). *What Does Justice Look Like? The Struggle for Liberation in Dakota Homeland*. St. Paul, MN: Living Justice Press, 2008.

Williams, Michael. *Americans and Their Forests: A Historical Geography*. Cambridge, UK: Cambridge University Press, 1992.

———. *Deforesting the Earth: From Prehistory to Global Crisis, An Abridgment*. London: University of Chicago Press, 2010.

Yaryan, Willie, Denzil Verardo and Jennie Verardo. *2000 Sempervirens Story: A Century of Preserving California's Ancient Redwood Forest 1900–2000*. Los Altos, CA: Sempervirens Fund, 2000.

Thesis/Dissertation

Long, Robert James. "Fresno County, California, and the Morrill Land Act of 1862: The Effects of William S. Chapman and Other Speculators upon Early-day Development." PhD diss., California State University, 1997.

Lybeck, Rick. "Fear and Reconciliation: The U.S.–Dakota War in White Public Pedagogy." PhD diss., University of Minnesota, 2015.

Yaryan, Willie. "Saving the Redwoods: The Ideology and Political Economy of Nature Preservation." PhD diss., University of California, Santa Cruz, 2002.

Articles

Andrews, Candice Gaukel. "Conservation or Preservation: Which Is Best for Now and in the Future?" *Good Nature Travel: The Official Travel Blog of Natural Habitat Adventures*, February 2020. https://www.nathab.com/blog/conservation-or-preservation-which-is-best-for-now-and-in-the-future.

Bliss, Traci, and Randall Brown. "The Saratoga Road to Big Basin." In *Redwood Logging and Conservation in the Santa Cruz Mountains: A Split History.* Edited by Lisa Robinson, 135–37. Santa Cruz, CA: Santa Cruz Museum of Art & History at the McPherson Center, 2014.

———. "Saving Big Basin Heroes and Heroines." In *Redwood Logging and Conservation in the Santa Cruz Mountains: A Split History*. Edited by Lisa Robinson, 117–28. Santa Cruz, CA: Santa Cruz Museum of Art & History at the McPherson Center, 2014.

Christensen, Terry, and Larry Gerston. "The Rise of the McClatchy's and Other Newspaper Dynasties." *The Californians: The Magazine of California History*, September/October 1983.

Eldredge, Zoeth Skinner. "Banking in California." In *History of California.* Vol. V. Edited by Zoeth Skinner Eldredge, 423–57. New York: Century History Company, 1915.

———. "San Francisco: The Earthquake and Fire of 1906." In *History of California*. Vol. V. Edited by Zoeth Skinner Eldredge, 505–21. New York: Century History Company, 1915.

Everett, Wallace. "Lumber Men and the Crisis Told." *Sunset Magazine*, April 1907.

Hodder, Sam. "Reckoning with League Founders' Eugenics Past." *Save the Redwoods League*, September 2020. https://www.savetheredwoods.org/blog/reckoning-with-the-league-founders-eugenics-past/.

Holder, C.F. "How a Forest Fire Was Extinguished with Wine." *Wide World Magazine,* August 1900.

Horton, Debbie. "About the Author." In *Quicksilver County Parks News,* Newsletter of the New Almaden Quicksilver Park Association, Spring 2003, 7–8.

Hull, Elizabeth. "Redwood in the 1906 San Francisco Earthquake." *Forest History Society Today,* Spring/Fall 2016.

Jones, Louise. "First Impressions." In *California Redwood Park.* Edited by Arthur A. Taylor, 28–33. Sacramento, CA: W. Richardson, 1912.

McCracken, Josephine. "About the Big Basin." *Overland Monthly,* August 1900, 135–39.

Nolan, Monica. "The Half Breed." *San Francisco Silent Film Festival Essay,* 2013.

Sleeper, Aric. "Pillars of the Earth: Remembering the Resilience of our Coast Redwoods." *The Santa Cruz Waves: Live the Lifestyle,* December/January 2021. Interview with Sandy Lydon.

Stanford, Leland. Governor's Speech of January 10, 1862, governors.library. ca.gov.

Pardee, George C. "Conservation in California." In *History of California.* Vol. V., 363–94. New York: Century History Company, 1915.

Pamphlets and Unpublished Documents

Bender, Allison C. "Valuable People: The Rise and Fall of the Lake Pepin Half-Breed Tract." History 489: Research Seminar, University of Wisconsin, 2016. https://minds.wisconsin.edu/bitstream/handle/1793/76065/Bender%2C%20Allison_2016%20Fall.pdf?sequence=2&isAllowed=y

Brown, Randall. "Paper Trail of Tears." Unpublished manuscript, August 2020.

Gibson, Ross Eric. "A History of De Laveaga and His Park." Unpublished manuscript, 2001.

Horton, Debbie. "About the Author." *Quicksilver County Parks News* (Spring 2003): 7–8.

Johnson, Frederick L. "'Half-Breed' Tract." *MNOpedia,* July 2013. http://www.mnopedia.org/place/half-breed-tract.

Jones, Louise Coffin. *Travel Journals of Early Life, Jones Family Collection.*

Book Reviews

LaBatte, John. "Review of *The Great Treasure of the Fort Snelling Prison Camp* by William Millikan." *Minnesota History Magazine*, Spring 2010. https://dakotawar1862.wordpress.com/2013/05/03/review-the-great-treasure/.

Sweet, Jimmy (Jameson). "Review of *Massacre in Minnesota: The Dakota War of 1862, the Most Violent Ethnic Conflict in American History* by Gary Clayton Anderson". *H-CivWar, H-Net Reviews* (April 2020). http://www.h-net.org/reviews/showrev.php?id=54350.

Journals

Gates, Paul W. "Public Land Disposal in California." *Agricultural History* 49, no. 1 (1975): 158–78.

Merchant, Carolyn. "Gender and Environmental History." *Journal of American History* 76, no. 4 (1990): 1,117–21.

Millikan, William. "The Great Treasure of the Fort Snelling Prison Camp." *Minnesota History* 62, no. 1 (Spring 2010): 4–15.

Sweet, Jimmy (Jameson). "Native Suffrage: Race, Citizenship, and Dakota Indians in the Upper Midwest." *Journal of the Early Republic* 11, no. 1 (Spring 2019): 99–109.

Archive Collection

William Russel Dudley Papers (SC0558). Department of Special Collections and University Archives, Stanford University Libraries, Stanford, California. Box 2: folder 20, 27; box 3: folder 14, 15, 18; box 4: folder 8; box 5: folder 11; box 17: folder 4.

Newspapers

Berkeley Gazette, 1906
Evening Sentinel, 1901, 1902, 1904, 1906, 1907
Mercury News (San Jose), 1900, 1910
Mountain Echo, 1900, 1908

Overland Monthly, 1900

Record-Union (Sacramento), 1887, 1894

Sacramento Bee, 1901, 1902, 1908, 1912

San Francisco Bulletin, 1891

San Francisco Call, 1895, 1900, 1901, 1902, 1908

San Francisco Chronicle, 1900, 1902, 1908

San Francisco Examiner, 1883, 1900, 1902

San Jose Evening News, 1901, 1902, 1904

Santa Cruz Evening News, 1910, 1911, 1921, 1922, 1925, 1926, 1928, 1929, 1934

Santa Cruz Sentinel, 1884, 1892, 1898, 1900, 1901, 1902, 1907, 1908, 1910, 1911, 1915, 1955

Santa Cruz Surf, 1883, 1891, 1897, 1889, 1892, 1893, 1897, 1899, 1900, 1901, 1902

Santa Cruz Weekly Sentinel, 1907

Interviews

Three individuals (Harold Hyde, Hopi Barrowclough and Barbara Young Stewart) who knew Jennie Bliss Jeter provided detailed historical context about her and William T. Jeter's life.

Jennie's grandnephew, Harold (aka Hal) Hyde of Watsonville, gave me many hours of his recollections in 2018.

Jennie's friend Hopi Barrowclough (born Doris Hopkins) was the granddaughter of Milo Hopkins, proprietor of Hopkins' Big Trees (aka Hopkins' Café), adjacent to Welches Big Trees Grove. (Milo Hopkins had been Jennie's trusted friend and farrier.) Hopi grew up at Hopkins' Big Trees, today part of Henry Cowell Redwood State Park, and took me on three extended walks there in 2011. She put key events and relationships that took place at the park between 1925 and 1955—related to preserving the trees—in their natural context.

Jennie's grandniece, Barbara Young Stewart of Piedmont, offered her perspective on Jennie's early life, loss of her child and many pertinent details such as her choice for the Jeter Tree during a 2012 interview.

Those individuals interviewed for the epilogue during 2021 are listed in the acknowledgements.

INDEX

ABOUT THE AUTHORS

 **Emerita Professor Traci Bliss** spent the first part of her career in state-level public policy positions beginning at the California Energy Commission in the late 1970s as the coordinator for solar energy education programs. She went on to become an award-winning education professor and state policy advisor to the National Board for Professional Teaching Standards. She holds a bachelor of arts (art history), master of arts (history/social studies) and PhD (education) from Stanford University and a master of public administration (public affairs) from the LBJ School, University of Texas at Austin. With this multidisciplinary lens, she captures the true story of Big Basin. A member of the Santa Cruz Historic Preservation Commission, her other recent books include the often-neglected role of women in community and environmental history. Bliss's ancestors William and Jennie Bliss Jeter were instrumental in saving Big Basin and in creating the county park that became Henry Cowell Redwoods State Park. As a docent at the park, she offers historic walking tours and helps train new docents. She continues the family tradition of community service as a third-generation member of Santa Cruz Rotary, which her grandfather helped found in 1922. You can find more about Traci's work at tracibliss.com.

Martin Rizzo-Martínez is the state park historian for the Santa Cruz District. He has taught at UC–Santa Cruz, Cabrillo College and to high-security inmates in Salinas Valley State Prison through Hartnell College. He is the author of a book on Santa Cruz Native history, *We Are Not Animals* (University of Nebraska Press, 2021).

Mark G. Hylkema is the supervisor of the Cultural Resources Program for thirty-two parks in the Santa Cruz District, California State Parks. He has forty years of experience in California archaeology, is the tribal liaison for the district and has taught at UC–Santa Cruz, Santa Clara University, Cabrillo, Ohlone and Foothill Colleges. (For Mark's work at Big Basin in 2021, see color insert section.)

Bonny Hawley is the executive director of Friends of Santa Cruz State Parks, where a dedicated team partners with California State Parks to operate thirty-two parks and beaches. Friends and State Parks are working together with the community to create California's newest state historic park at the Castro Adobe.

Visit us at
www.historypress.com